PANACHE
and the Art of Faking It

PANACHE
and the
Art of Faking It

How to make the greatest impression
on the largest number of people
in the shortest period of time.

by

BOB LEVINE

Illustrated by

PETER STEINER

COMMUNICATIONS, INC.

New York

The author would like to thank Leonard Brice, Nancy Bruning, Sheila Feldman, Michael Ross and Billy Mernit for their contributions. Without them, well, you know.

Published in Canada by Methuen Publications, 2330 Midland Avenue, Agincourt, Ontario M1S 1P7

Library of Congress Cataloging in Publication Data
Levine, Bob, 1944-
    Panache and the art of faking it.

        1. Conduct of life.   2. Success.   3. Etiquette.
I. Title.
BJ1581.2.L477   1982   158'.1'0207   82-50716
ISBN 0-943392-01-2
CANADIAN ISBN: 0-458-95580-9
Written by Bob Levine
All illustrations by Peter Steiner
Designed by Jacques Chazaud

Printed in the United States of America

First Edition: September 1982

    2 3 4 5 6 7 8 9 10

Contents ▬▬▬▬▬

Savoir dissimuler est le savoir des rois.
(Dissimulation is the art of kings.)

ARMAND JEAN DU PLESSIS
DUC DE RICHELIEU
Mirame

Introduction ═══════════

*W*elcome to the Age of Unenlightenment.

Who today has time to be casually conversant about the latest in architectural design, the newest breakthrough in computer technology, the baby genius of cinema verité?

No one.

Yet just imagine how great it would be if you could chat knowingly about next week's entries at Epsom, the silly little mistake in the computer room that's going to cost the company millions or the tiny but charming vineyard in Sonoma where they're bottling a truly magnificent Blanc de Blanc.

The solution?

Five more years at grad school?

A live-in tutor?

Eight thousand dollars worth of reference books?

Not at all.

What you need is panache, conveyed by knights of old by a white plume on their helmets and defined then as now, as "a dashing elegance of manner"—plus the art of faking it. *You supply the first. We supply the second.*

The best of information when hesitantly conveyed is received with skepticism—HOW you display your facts is as important as the facts themselves.

A few of you may opt to follow in the footsteps of medieval tradition by affixing a white plume to your porkpie, your beanie or your snood. But the vast majority of you will sport your plume in imagination only, relying on a repertoire of appropriate smiles, frowns, shrugs and sneers to show that you too have mastered a "dashing elegance of manner."

Chances are you'll need to practice. Be diligent. While dressing in the morning, driving to the unemployment office, breaking away on the stationary bicycle over at the gym . . . . keep practicing.

Once your style of delivery is perfected, all that remains is to commit this book to memory. I did. You can too.

The Author

1
Eat, Drink, and Be Merry

Booze

. . . how to order the right stuff

Yes, booze. Gone are the days when you could walk into a bar and simply order a vodka and tonic or a bourbon on the rocks. Brand names are part and parcel of the performance and ritual, and the most improbably lengthy conversations now take place about, Lord help us, Polish vodka. And you certainly don't want to get caught with your highball glass around your ankles, or whatever that expression is. And so, listen and learn.

Let's get vodka out of the way. All of it still smells vaguely like mimeograph-machine fluid (remember running off leaflets in high school?) if you can notice the smell at all, but its smell is its least important aspect. Because, as liquors go, vodka is so boring (what else can you mix with juice, tabasco, worcestershire sauce, salt, pepper, horseradish, and celery and still call booze?) it actually requires the greatest amount of time to discuss. The first important thing to mention, often and loud, is that all domestic vodkas taste the same. This is true, and spare us any conversation about charcoal filtering or the lack thereof. Keep the conversation to eighty-proof vodkas, since the higher-proof ones can make you crazy anyway.

The thing about imported vodkas is that they actually have a taste, a taste of something other than alcohol. Stolichnaya (one orders "Stoly on the rocks, with a piece of lime" unless it's already chilled, in which case a small snifter will do, or a wine glass) is the finest of Russian vodkas — Smirnoff is *not* Russian — and has a slightly sweet taste, though not enough for an untrained palate to notice. Should you be boycotting things Russian, Finlandia will be your next choice (or perhaps your first, if you're "tired" of Stoly), and you drink it the same way, or in a *very* dry martini. Wyborova, the Polish vodka that tastes oddly like gasoline and somehow manages to make people drunker faster, should be drunk ice cold as well, but with some freshly ground pepper on top. The heartburn factor here is very high, but it always throws people off and dazzles them with your panache. It also tastes good. Tsingtao, a Chinese vodka, is great for exotica and one-upmanship, but it tastes like small pieces of the Great Wall have fallen into it. Sweden's Absolut vodka is becoming très chic, and indeed it's wonderful, if a bit too fashionable. There's also a Turkish vodka, which tastes like carpets, and you needn't concern yourself with it. There ought, by the way, to be a law against putting orange juice or other colorful liquids in these vodkas, so don't become part of a crime statistic.

The subject of scotches is far simpler. Scotch is rarely sullied the way vodka is, and so "how to order" is not really an issue here. If you prefer your scotch with ginger ale or cola, please move on to the next chapter. If not, pay heed.

The greatest snob-appeal scotches are Laphroaig, Glenlivet, and Glenfiddich. They are all dense, taste vaguely like grainy malteds, are expensive, and should be drunk neat (no ice). It is always nice to order one of them after one of your tablemates (or barmates) has ordered, with the epic pretension that comes with a little bit of knowledge (far less than you're getting here), "Dewar's, please, in a tall glass, two ice cubes, and a splash" or "Teacher's, a touch of soda, no ice." Those folks think they've got "taste," but a simple "Laphroaig, neat," from you will put an end to the question of who has the most panache.

If you must drink bourbon, as some must, make it JD. JD is the only thing rednecks and advertising account executives have in common, and should be treasured as such. You will, of course, have to explain that you know that Jack Daniel's isn't *really* bourbon — it has something to do with the way it's distilled and is none of your business unless moonshining is your hobby — but that it's so much better than any real bourbon that it has become even more, well, *bourbonish*. You drink it neat, and if you're really looking to impress some heavies (in the bulk sense of heavy), a beer chaser will do. It's nauseating, you'll fall down drunk, it's hardly elegant — but it will shut up the people sitting in the Texas-like boozery you've wound up in. And it will make the account executives really sit up and play with their calculators.

These are out:

- blended whiskeys
- Harvey Wallbangers (If you don't know, don't ask.)
- anything green, sticky, or thick
- Brandy Alexanders, unless you're making some bizarre point
- special gins, like Bombay or Tanqueray (Either drink gin, or don't.)
- tequila, except for Cuervo Gold
- cheap brandy (If you can't afford the good stuff, drink it anyway.)
- Calvados, Grand Marnier, Drambuie — except after dinner or before seductions
- grapefruit juice and *anything*
- specifying a particular brand and accepting another if the bar or restaurant doesn't have it (better to switch liquors than compromise).

TO YOUR HEALTH!

Wine ═══════════════

... *here's looking at you, kid*

*A*n interesting fact: Only about fourteen people in the world actually know as much about wine as they claim to. The multitudes who say things like "It has a witty bouquet" and "This particular red has mellowed since last year, but it's still somewhat arrogant" are faking it. Yes, they know red from white, very good from vinegar, and that it's nasty to throw ice cubes into glasses that contain the sixty dollars a bottle red wine they were given as an anniversary gift by a business associate who could think of nothing else to buy them. But five will get you ten that they don't know nearly as much as they sound like they know. The attitude here is consummate verve — better known as panache.

In the eventuality that *you* are put in the position of an expert (as is befitting your station) or must compete with a blowhard, there are several ways you can rise to the occasion. Smiling smugly won't get you anywhere, nor will turning the choice over to your opponent. People who are supposed to know their wines welcome the chance to prove it. The following tips and facts will not only get you by, they will strike a sort of awe in your dinner companions or cocktail party co-conversationalists.

Expensive wine is not necessarily better than cheap wine, it's merely harder to criticize. If you've commited a large sum of money to a bottle that four people can't even get high on, you tend to accept your fate and learn to like it.

Red is for meat, white is for fish and poultry — except if you want to be purposefully perverse. This is acceptable if said with panache and authority and you don't order a *specific* wine to go with the "wrong" food. Beaujolais is good with anything, and everyone waits for the new batch each year. It's *almost* always better than last year's, but not nearly as good as the one two or three years ago. (You'll never be challenged on this: no one remembers a Beaujolais for more than a year.) Don't bother learning about rosés; nice people don't drink them.

If you swallow your mouthful while your tablemates are still sloshing theirs around (a silly ritual at best), you'll be one up. You can comment on the aftertaste first, i.e., "Wow, this has some aftertaste" or "The aftertaste is really surprising!"

Sweet wines are better called "dessert" wines, and you don't like them for the most part. The exception is Château d'Yquem (pronounced dee-kem), which is the greatest, is brutally expensive, and "it was like drinking amber" last time you had it. You never bought it; it was given to you as a gift and you saved it for a really special occasion.

It's always good to discuss prices in a general manner. Saying that there really is no difference between a four dollar and an eight dollar bottle of wine and that to get real quality one must go much higher is a case in point. Try to find a decent four dollar wine and tout it whenever possible — "best value for the money," etc. Do not believe your liquor store merchant; he's there to sell wine. If he tells you something is a "really good table wine and inexpensive," you may repeat that verbatim.

Burgundies are more "hearty and full bodied" than Bordeaux; '61, '66, and '75 were superb years for Bordeaux. It's that simple.

Drinking spritzers (wine with soda) is a crime, except for women coming out of a swimming pool. If you must make one, make it with Folinari, an okay, cheap white wine. Summers only. Red spritzers don't exist in your world. Look surprised and register disbelief that one would not only dilute, but chill a red wine.

Should you be challenged after tasting and giving your opinion, shrug and say politely, "Do you really think so?" That should do the trick.

California wines are winning blind taste tests against French wines more and more often. "Ridge wines are going up in price," you say, and "are vastly more interesting than French wines, which simply don't have the character California wines have developed." Try to see to it that the person with whom you are talking isn't from California, since wine is their only cultural event and they are therefore all "experts" on the subject. This is a good conversation to hold with people from other countries.

One rarely prefers one color wine over the other. You might "not be in the mood" for white for a few months, however. There seems to be more "variety" in red wines in general, and sometimes white is just "too light."

To say that a bottle is "corked" is not to imply that it's either open or closed. It means that something weird has happened and the wine has gone bad (say "The bottle is bad"), having something to do with the air or the way the wine was stored (standing up or on its head, not lying down). It will taste noticeably bad and you will send it back.

The ONLY reason for sending wine back in a restaurant is if it has "turned" (gone bad). If you don't like it, it's your fault — you chose it. If everyone at the table is displeased and you ordered it, mention that it's an acquired taste, grin, drink it, and order a different bottle for them. It's not your fault if their palates aren't as sophisticated as yours.

Red wines have to "breathe" before they are served, and it doesn't matter why. This means either opening the bottle and letting it sit, or putting it into a wider-necked decanter and letting it sit. "This wine has to breathe for quite a while" (two hours) can imply real quality if said right.

Port wine (served after dinner, in the library, with cigars) has to be at least forty years old to be any good. Too much new or cheap port will give the worst hangover imaginable. No one in this day and age springs for the good stuff; if they do, they don't let anyone drink enough of it to make them ill.

The greatest Clarets (red Bordeaux) are Margaux, Lafite-

Rothschild, Latour. The '76 Lafite is about fifty dollars a bottle. If it's offered, you take it graciously.

As you can see, it's incredibly easy to be wine savvy. Should you be faced with a genuine expert (one of the fourteen), he or she won't give you a chance to express your opinion anyway. Just agree with the pronouncement (eyes closed for a split second), lick your lips, and softly say, "mmm."

Les Plus Ultra French Restaurants ═══

... how to get a table when you don't have a reservation and the place is fully booked

Y ou're in Chicago or New York on business. Someone — or several people — who can do you a great deal of professional good want to go to Le Français or Lutéce. You wish to impress them with your consummately cosmopolitan aplomb and power. The restaurateurs in question don't know you from a hole in the ground, but you're certainly not going to let your business associate know that. The restaurants have been booked a month in advance. You have until the following evening. What do you do? Panic? Say you're allergic to French food? Bah! You get into the restaurant. And you do it with panache — sometimes known as *chutzpah.*

It is crucial to remember whom you are dealing with here. The French like an authoritative voice, they like to be flattered, and they like to be groveled to — not necessarily in that order. All French chef-owners know each other, too, so if you know one (or claim to), another will treat you like an honored guest, especially if you explain that Chef A simply made you promise you would eat at Chef B's place when you were in town. As we said, you have one day. Call the restaurant:

RESTAURANT: *Bon soir*, may I help you?

YOU: Yes, my name is Stewart and I'm calling to confirm my reservation for tomorrow evening and to change it from three to four people (or vice versa — any other change means a different size table and is rude to suggest).

RESTAURANT: (after a pause) I'm sorry Mr. Stewart, we don't seem to have any reservation in that name.

YOU: (slightly perturbed) Well, that's not my fault. I made the reservation myself almost a month ago and I will only be here for another day. What do you suggest I do?

You are now past the "authoritative voice" stage. You have his ear, but he is not about to help you. You continue.

YOU: I simply won't go to another restaurant when I'm in [city]. I can still remember the perfect dinner I had a couple of weeks ago when I was with those five Japanese businessmen. They said it was the high point of their visit to the United States, and I'm certain it was.

You have now gotten to "flattery" and the suggestion that you spent hundreds of dollars on your last meal there. He is beginning to perk up.

> You: (with a slight whine in your voice) Isn't there anything you can do for me? Check your reservations once again? Put me on a waiting list? Any hour tomorrow evening would be fine, even though I specifically made the reservation for eight o'clock.

You have now begun to grovel, all the while holding firm to your original statement — that you had a reservation to begin with. You will, in fact, be put on a waiting list and told to call back the following day — which you will obediently do, and often. If you should speak to another person the following day, explain to him/her that the person you spoke with the day before had virtually promised you a table for that evening. And don't worry, you'll get in.

Another ploy involves calling, once again, to *confirm*, using a heavy South American or British accent and claiming you are the secretary to Señor and Mrs. Argento, or Lord and Lady Winston. When faced with the inevitable, i.e., there is no reservation, mention your call from your "native" land well over a month ago and state that you hope there hasn't been a mix-up. (Stage 1 — authoritative voice.) The meal at their restaurant means everything to your employers — they always eat there, often under other names, to avoid being recognized. They only eat the best, hence their frequent visits. (Stage 2 — flattery.) If you still haven't been put on a waiting list or been confirmed, remember Stage 3, groveling. Explain that you will lose your job if the mix-up turns out to be your fault, and beg them to try really hard to accommodate your employers. Follow above instructions for the following day's calls.

The final attack is one that requires a bit of easy research. You must know the names of two chefs, cities apart. As we mentioned earlier, they all know and respect each other, and so it is your job to tell Chef A that Chef B had promised *to make the reservation for you himself and you simply can't believe he forgot.* Trust us, what with making sauces out of partridge lungs and the like, they don't have time to call each other to confirm. Refer to Chef B by his first name, and the chef to whom you are talking as "monsieur." Authority, flattery, and just a touch of groveling again will do the trick.

Cooking and Eating

... you in the kitchen, you at the table

*E*ach of us secretly considers himself/herself a good cook and a better eater, with wonderfully varied tastes. We shrug modestly while admitting that our lasagna is world-revered, and invite our host and hostess wholeheartedly "some time" for our veal with peppers, mushrooms, and marsala, all the while praising to the skies what we are eating at the moment. The problem arises, therefore, as to how to keep the conversation in your court (kitchen or field of expertise, so to speak) so that you can sound like a real expert, even if barbequed chickens are really your favorite things to cook and eat. If it's ever possible to be esoteric and simple at the same time, this is it. There are, first of all, things *not* to do.

Do not:

- brag about your quiche (this has-been has become as commonplace as cold breakfast cereal)
- serve "pigs-in-blankets" at stand-up cocktail parties
- prefer restaurants with salad bars (in fact, you'd be wise to have never heard of them)
- even acknowledge the existence of iceberg lettuce

- mention coq au vin or boeuf bourguignon in a discussion of French food (these dishes were okay fifteen years ago but now are in the same category as quiche)
- make a face or throw up at the mention of escargots (while they are no longer considered exotic — and so liking them won't get you high points — being appalled by them is gauche and will give you away instantly)
- put ketchup on lamb
- prefer all your Italian food with red sauce
- salt your food before you taste it.
- ask for a side order of fries or MSG

Now that those are out of the way, here are some pieces of knowledge, bluffs and attitudes to make you sound like a mini Julia Child or James Beard.

- When you are served your salad with a fancy dressing, announce your preference for "the perfect vinaigrette,"

which only you and a few restaurateurs in the south of France know how to make. It consists of (you are willing to share the secret) olive oil, expensive vinegar (Balsamic is the best — and should be for four dollars a bottle) and a dab of Dijon or other French mustard. Hold the spices. Period.

- Say something like, "Coriander is the most misunderstood of herbs."
- If anchovies make you sick (which is only right), say you don't like them because they bury the taste of everything they're served with.
- State your newfound preference for American caviar — the gold-colored sturgeon caviar. It's very chic and much cheaper than Iranian or Russian, which you're boycotting anyway.
- Praise small, undecorated Chinese restaurants that are cheap.
- Undercook all vegetables.
- Serve pepper and salt from a dish or a mill, *not a shaker*.
- Only want Mexican or Indian food occasionally. The former "deadens the palate"; the latter "is never prepared properly in this country — they simply can't seem to get the right spices here."
- Regardless of what you're being served, ask your table-mates if they've ever tried adding a touch of vinegar to it while it's cooking. It always sounds like a good idea.
- If you must serve dessert, opt for fruit and cheese (a runny Brie and something no one else likes will do) instead of butterscotch ice cream (or *anyone's* flavor of the month/week/day) with chocolate syrup.

You are now prepared for the finest restaurant/dining room/kitchen conversation. Of course, you will never cook for anyone, mostly because you're waiting for your new cookware from France, along with it the imported tarragon in sealed tubes. If you *never* want to talk about cooking, plead total ignorance and explain how the family cook never allowed you in her kitchen when you were a child. End of *that* discussion, and with great style to boot!

Health Food ═══════════

. . . getting in with the mung bean and soy set

The question that immediately springs to mind is Why bother? Health-food addicts are a notoriously humorless, if healthy, lot. But if you have ever been in their company, the lone degenerate among these paragons of clean living, you know the answer. These energetic bundles of unsullied protein have a knack for making you feel like something that crawled out from under a rock. While normally content as an unrepentant Oreo lover, when placed among bran worshippers all your resolve seems to dissolve in a puddle of self-doubt. To help you through these times of trouble here are some tips and catch phrases. These chestnuts-to-be are to endear you to all but the most hardened health nuts.

Mea Culpa. The basic rule of thumb: *If it tastes good, it is bad for you.* Similarly: *The worse it tastes, the better it is for you.* Twinkies, taco chips, even toast ("burns out the vitamins") are no-nos. You claim to snack on raw carrots and vile concoctions such as brewer's yeast and wheat germ oil mixed with goat's milk. Meat in general is out — "It makes you mean, man" and interferes with your mellowness. Organically fed chickens are a possibility (try to avoid cracks about them being fed brown rice and bean sprouts; it is probably true and therefore, not funny). Professing pure vegetarianism for either humanitarian or health reasons is best, but if you must confess to eating foods that reside outside the vegetarian arena, claim that you stick to fish and avoid red meat. This would *seem* to make fast food burgers okay, since that meat (if it is meat) is probably far from red when it is finally cooked, but this is not the case.

Another rule: If it makes you feel good, it is bad for you. No caffeine, nicotine, or alcohol allowed. You may be amazed at how many health-food freaks smoke, but keep in mind that one is not allowed to justify the act on the grounds that cigarettes are "vegetable matter."

Haute cuisine. Forget it! The epitome of culinary art in the world of health foods is the spinach salad. Anything else is too oily (bad for the skin), too rich (bad for the arteries), too spicy (bad for the stomach), or causes cancer. Creative cooking becomes difficult when the most exotic spice permitted is lemon juice. You may be assured of adulation from your "peers" by knowing twenty-five ways to prepare alfalfa sprouts (avec sauce chocolat is not allowed); you'll score extra points for growing your own in a hydroponic tank in the basement.

Vitamins A-Z. A shortcut or short circuit, if you will, to any conversation about vitamins is to maintain, "I never take vitamin capsules, I get all I need naturally in my diet" and "Between brown rice and mung beans I get them all." Since one person's vitamin needs can be completely different from another's, almost any diet can be justified if pronounced confidently as "right for your system." "I live on bananas and bee pollen" said with just the right flair will sail you through any grilling on vitamin supplements.

Fasting. Not to be confused with dieting, one fasts not to lose weight but to "cleanse the system of impurities." Fasting can be used to gracefully get you out of eating proffered carrot-squash-and-soybean casserole when what you really want is a chunk of cheesecake. "I'm on a water fast" is a phrase guaranteed to set little health-food hearts aflutter and put the kabosh on any doubts as to your credentials.

Liquids. Tap water is taboo and Perrier is for parvenus. True health-food fanatics drink only water from mountain streams above 13,000 feet or acidophilus shakes (about which the less said the better). An office-sized water cooler in your home is considered adequate proof of your earnestness. Juices are acceptable, fruit or vegetable, but must be squeezed in your own juicer. Do not run out and buy one, however, because cleaning it is one of the labors of Hercules. If you are forced to entertain a devotee of the whole grain life, buy a small quantity of freshly made juice at the local health-food store and serve it as your own, ranting all the while about "how quickly the vitamins are lost."

Restaurants. Health-food restaurants are the pits. If possible steer the crowd to a Japanese restaurant. Japanese food is acceptable and differs from health food in that it is edible. If you are forced to go to a health-food restaurant, eat a steak before you leave the house — then you can order a bowl of miso soup and a grape and wow the assemblage with your "Eastern asceticism."

Faking one's way through the world of health foods is not all that difficult, because there is a certain amount of fakery already going on among the citizenry. A quick tour through any health-food store will reveal that attempts are being made to take the pain out of being healthy. You will spy health-food steaks, health-food cakes, health-food soda, health-food ice cream and, on your way out, a rack of health-food candy that would turn Mars & Co. green with envy.

Health-food types are at least subliminally aware that all is not right, and even the most hardened brown-rice junkie will occasionally down an entire box of chocolate doughnuts in a nervous fit. This thread of guilty secrets runs through all advocates of the Whole Foods Way, which is why you have an advantage. As a guiltless devourer of chemicals, insecticides, and carcinogens you have the upper hand in this game of one-upmanship. You can pontificate confidently on the joys of goats' milk yogurt, secure in the knowledge that you will never go near the stuff. Your attendants, on the other hand, will fear to press you on the issue lest you reveal that only last week you saw them furtively washing down hot dogs with beer!

2

Getting Yours

Making It With Women ═══

... undressing the feminine mystique

*T*he secret to faking it with women is understanding women. The secret to understanding women is the knowledge that while they are as different as snowflakes in most respects, in one way they are all alike — they are confused when it comes to men. One has only to watch such women as Mia Farrow and Elizabeth Taylor hop from Frank Sinatra to Woody Allen and from Richard Burton to Senator Warner (and beyond), respectively. Case closed. "No!" women cry, "we just have catholic tastes, unlike you men who stick to one type — endless permutations of your mother!" Not true (well, maybe there's a shred of something to the part about men and their mothers). Women vacillate between such extremes because they all secretly desire the same type — a hybrid of Richard Burton and Woody Allen.

It has been asked, "What do women want?" When it comes to men, the answer is, "They don't know!" On the one hand, they want someone who is safe, secure, modest, reliable, gentle, tender, and madly in love with them. On the other hand, they want a wild, impetuous, crazy, dangerous, roughneck romantic who basically doesn't care about them — *and* they want both to be the same person. "Impossible!" men cry, "no one but a schizo could be both, and even he wouldn't be both at the same time!" True, but any man contains the seeds of both John Wayne and a Monaco croupier despite the fact that he leans one way or the other most of the time. The secret to getting and holding a woman is to beef up the part that is not naturally your own personality, and to do this you must Fake It.

If you have the body of Burt Reynolds and John Paul Getty's money, as well as a Harley-Davidson 750 that you regularly drive into swimming pools, you probably have little trouble attracting women. Keeping them around is another story. Women may be confused, but they are not stupid. They know that your type goes through women like six-packs, and no girl wants to end up with the empty Buds, so they usually drop you before you drop them.

Your job is to throw them off guard. Just when they have got you pegged as a typical, macho, love-em-and-leave-em type, you burst into tears. When asked what is wrong, you say, "It's nothing, just free-floating anxiety; it will pass." While they are reeling from that, tell them that you are really "terrified of the void" and that your macho personality is just your "existential way of dealing with it." By the time they figure out that you don't know what you are talking about (assuming *they* do), you will be home free.

In art this is called "undercutting" — taking an obvious image and throwing a curve ball. Another example would be taking off your leather pants (your type should have no problem reaching this stage) to reveal hand monogrammed, custom made pure silk shorts. This upsets their preconceived image of you. In addition, women find androgyny extremely attractive (look at Bowie and Nureyev).

You "wild and crazy" types have less trouble getting women than holding on to them. When they start throwing your clothes out onto the street, it is your job to convince them that your philandering is *your* problem and is no threat to them. Try lines like, "I only fool around because I'm afraid I might be gay" or "I know I'm not good enough for you." (Try to say these things before she does, they are definitely more effective that way.) This, though, will only put off the inevitable. She will eventually dump you "for her own preservation" unless, of course, you actually do settle down, in which case she will dump you out of boredom — "You're not as much fun as you used to be."

If you are the quiet, stable type, you have trouble attracting women in the first place or else find that while you have a lot of women friends, you haven't had sex in five years. Your main problem is that you believe what women tell you — that they appreciate your sensitivity and warmth, and it is wonderful to be able to talk to you, "not like that crazy Jimmy or Frankie" (whom they only sleep with). They mean it — they do appreciate you — it is just that they take you for granted and find you about as sexually exciting as doing the laundry.

Well, it is easier than you think to change that. Try an occasional hint about some trouble before you met them: "A good friend died, but I'd rather not talk about it. . . ." Start showing up late (or better still, not at all) for dates with girls who "just want to be friends," but whom you would like to ravish. Explain the next day with, "Gee, I'm sorry, but she just wouldn't let me go," then immediately change the subject. No need to elaborate as to who "she" might be or why exactly she wouldn't let you go — let their imaginations do the work.

Best of all, get drunk, sloppy drunk, make a fool out of yourself, and be carried out of a bar — there is nothing like it for shocking platonic girlfriends out of their complacency. Once they begin to view you in this new light, it is but a short trip to the bedroom with this favorite former friend.

Once you are firmly ensconced as her lover and roommate, holding on is merely a matter of keeping her from getting bored and, once again, taking you for granted. Your naturally agreeable personality will keep her basically happy, but it doesn't hurt to occasionally stay out all night without calling. Be sure to come home with an incredibly flimsy excuse.

Women are actually easy to please. If you are Errol Flynn, temper it with a little *Father Knows Best*, and if you are essentially Wally Cox, give them a little *Wild One*. It is not necessary to change your basic personality, just spice it up with a little Dr. Jekyll or Mr. Hyde, whichever is needed. Remember, when Woody Allen gave Diane Keaton a little Bogey in *Play It Again Sam*, she fell for it . . . and him!

Making It With Men ═══════

. . . unexpurgated "how to" gospel

T he phone has stopped ringing. It seems like you haven't had a date since the junior prom. Why, you wonder? Could it be that you started snoring when Ralph was explaining the workings of his fuel-injected Ferrari? Or maybe it was because you burst into hysterics when John told you that he was having a lot of success with his brewer's yeast and bean sprout diet. "But I was just reacting honestly," you protest. This is fine if you enjoy the social life of a nun. But if you want the attentions of the male of the species, you will have to learn to behave with flair.

Lesson #1 — Humor

Only about 25 percent of the male population has anything remotely resembling a sense of humor, and of that group, only .006 percent have any sense of humor about themselves (in Europe, it is closer to .000000000006 percent). While you are expected to find even his oldest "knock knock" jokes hilarious, you must never under any circumstances laugh *at* a man.

When he tells you his first wife left him because he "was too much 'man' for her," awed sighs are appropriate; guffaws are not. When the two long strands of hair that he is combing across his otherwise bald head are blown by the wind so that they hang below his chin, try to focus on something of interest in his belt buckle until he rearranges them. Holding your sides and turning red in the face will not lead to dinners at the Four Seasons.

Lesson #2 — Sports

Yes, sports are boring, but they are very important to men, so you might as well understand them. It is unnecessary to actually watch the games broadcast on television, since everything of interest that happens during a game will be rebroadcast on the evening news. This is only possible because the largest part of any game is taken up with things like time-outs, halftimes, huddles, conferences on the pitcher's mound, etc. You must never, of course, say this to a man — to him, every minute of a game is as important as finding the cure for cancer.

If you are forced to watch a game with a man, feel free to read a book — the man will be too absorbed in the game to notice. You need only to look up during the commercials and when you hear the announcers going wild. They will then show an instant replay of whatever they were excited about, so you don't have to worry about missing anything.

Lesson #3 — Work

A man "is" what he "does." He takes his work very seriously and he loves to talk about it. If you are planning an evening with a CPA or an insurance salesman, drink a pot of coffee before he picks you up. Try to get him to take you to a movie or a concert — anywhere the opportunity for conversation is limited. A show of some kind will also give you a topic, other than his work, for discussion.

Do not expect to talk about *your* work — he will either assume that you are only doing it until Mister Right comes along, or, if you convince him that you are serious about your career, he will become instantly impotent. Which brings us to . . .

Lessons #4, 5, 6, 7, 8, 9 — Sex

A recent poll among males eighteen to sixty-five asked: True or False, "Men only want one thing." As you may have guessed, 98.2 percent answered *true.* Men are hypocrites about many things, but this is not one of them. They may lie to you, but rest assured they are not lying to themselves.

We are told that one-night stands are now okay for women. This is true if that is all you want from a guy. If, on the other hand, you meet a fellow who seems on the surface to be neither a creep, moron, momma's boy, nor a professional stud and you think you might want an ongoing relationship, hold out. Even if you want to tear his clothes off immediately — *control yourself.*

There is no need to put off sex until you are married, but

if you hop into bed shortly after "hello," it definitely reduces your air of mystery. Besides, many a "dreamboat" on the first date has turned into a garbage scow by the third. If you "go all the way" on the first date, there may not be a third, and you may lament the loss of someone who doesn't rate your tears. This may be starting to sound like Emily Post for young moderns, but it is true that for men the "grass is always greener." The longer you stay on the other side of the fence, the longer they will hang around.

When at last you have consummated the relationship, he will ask, "How was it for you?" If you desire ever to see this man again, you must resist the urge to say things like, "It was better than polio" or "How was what?" *Lie!!* Say, "The earth moved" — he won't laugh (see Lesson #1 **Humor,** above). Say he "is the best." Everyone else has lied, and if you don't think so, it is *your* problem.

The truth of the matter is that no matter what they say, men do not want to hear the truth. Tell him, "That plaid jacket and striped pants combination is so distinctive — so *you*." Tell him, "Actuarial science has always been a secret fascination of mine." Tell him, "Virgo, what's yours" and "That's alright, it happens to everyone." If you don't have the stomach for it — well, there's always the convent.

3

Aural Gratification

Classical Music ════════

. . . what you like, what you don't

*F*lat statements are the order of the day here. They imply vast knowledge. Herewith, fourteen classics.

- Beethoven's symphonies 3, 5, 7, and 9 are the best. The sixth is also fine, but 1, 2, 4, and 8 are not as inspired.
- Of LVB's five piano concertos ("concerti" is correct but it is a bit much), the fifth is the most famous and popular. You prefer the fourth. It is greater.
- Ravel's *Bolero* and Tchaikovsky's *1812 Overture* are both stupid pieces of music, despite Bo Derek and the Fourth of July.
- Mozart was perfect. Everything he wrote (forty-one symphonies, twenty-seven piano concertos, hundreds of other works) is worth listening to.
- You don't listen to Tchaikovsky. He is for children and the ballet.
- Handel's *Messiah* is great despite its popularity. You prefer it performed as it is written, with a small orchestra and chorus. New arrangements make it sound like a small war.
- J.S. Bach was a humble, religious man. All of his sons who lived became composers, the best of which was Carl Philipe Emanuel Bach. You like all of J.S. Bach's music but "have trouble with" the suites for solo cello. This, you readily admit, is a flaw of yours. In fact, it is your only flaw, musically.
- Schubert's *Unfinished Symphony* (the eighth) is as finished as he wanted it to be. He died young, like Mozart.

- Haydn is dull except for choral music. He wrote 104 symphonies, the last twelve of which you can tolerate.
- You are sick of Brahms.
- Modern music is impossible to listen to. Those guys just write for other musicians, not the public.
- Some Stravinsky is great, e.g. *The Symphony of Psalms*. His ballet *Le Sacre Du Printemps* caused a riot in Paris in 1910.
- You love thirteenth-to-fifteenth century music scored for choir and brass that was written to be performed in churches in Venice. It is "joyful, yet solemn."
- You love the Chicago Symphony and Cleveland Orchestra. You do not like the Boston Pops.

Allow other people to talk and then change the subject to one of the above. Speak enthusiastically, and with the right combination of reverance and verve.

Jazz, Man

. . . Nat Hentoff, watch out

*L*et's face it, to be a true member of the jazz cognoscenti you should be at least part black. If you cannot arrange this, don't despair — you can still command a great deal of respect among the terminally hip. It's just a matter of artfully sprinkling your conversation with a few choice tidbits.

You must remember that there are only two types of jazz: mainstream and avant-garde. Jazz-rock or fusion is now derisively called *fuzak*, and no one cares about it anymore. Mainstream jazz is any style in which all the musicians play in the same key and time signature. In avant-garde jazz such considerations take a poor second to being angry and black. Any white avant-garde players can be dismissed, as they themselves are faking it.

Depending on which camp you are addressing feel free to use the following pontifications.

You are mainstream speaking to avant-garde. "That stuff doesn't communicate, it is musical masturbation" or less heavy-handedly, "That stuff may be fun to play but it is impossible to listen to." (Do not preface sentences with "like"; no one has talked that way since 1963. However, "man" used judiciously is still acceptable.)

You are avant-garde speaking to mainstream. "That stuff is no longer relevant to the Black Experience." This takes nerve if you are white, so you may want to limit yourself to, "Hasn't that ground already been sufficiently covered?"

If you don't want to stop the conversation quite that dead, you will need to know the following.

Unlike rock, there are few if any "bands" in jazz. (Weather Report is a notable exception.) Players group and regroup with the regularity of a suburban "swap" club, and you can't tell the players without a score card, so here is a score card to help you pretend that you know who's who and what's happenin'.

Saxophone. John Coltrane: 'Trane is God for both mainstream and avant alike. You "love *Ascension*" (the album) but "can't listen to it very often" (most people can't listen to it at all), however you feel *Ballads* is "secretly his best album." You love Charlie Parker, Lester Young ("Prez"), Gene Ammons ("Jug"), Sonny Rollins, and Wayne Shorter (with Miles, *not* Weather Report).

If you dig avant, it's Albert Ayler, Eric Dolphy, and Ornette Coleman.

Piano. McCoy Tyner, a former Coltrane sideman, you claim "has never made a bad album." Thelonius Monk was as holy as his name implies. Chick Corea (not to be confused with North or South Korea) is "best as a composer" and you "liked his group *Return to Forever*, pre and post guitars." As for Keith Jarrett, either you "admire his love of the piano as a sole acoustic instrument" or you consider him to be "the biggest wanker" (an English term for someone who specializes in self-abuse) you have ever heard; there is no middle ground with Keith. You love (mainstream) Lennie Tristano, Bill Evans, Art Tatum, Cedar Walton, Herbie Hancock (pre and post fusion), and Steve Kuhn. For the avant, Cecil Taylor stands out and alone.

Bass. The late Charlie Mingus is the legend in residence, more as a composer and musical genius than as a technician. *Negative* points will be awarded for being into or even aware of Joni Mitchell's album tribute to him. Ron Carter "hasn't done much since the Miles quintet days" (see Miles, below). Stanley Clarke "was great at nineteen, but he picked up an electric bass and his taste went out the window." You love, for mainstream, Eddie Gomez and Charlie Haden. There are no avant bass players worth worrying about.

Trumpet. Miles and Dizzy, Dizzy and Miles, they are all ye know and all ye need know. Miles Davis (never actually use his full name or the jig is up) made some of the greatest jazz albums ever recorded. You love *Miles Smiles* and *E.S.P.* and, "yes, his seminal fusion album *Bitches Brew* was great, but God, what crimes have been committed in its name." Dizzy Gillespie, always Dizzy or Diz, wrote the classic *Night in Tunisia* and is "technically phenomenal," the "be-bop master." Freddie Hubbard "used to be good" and "can still play when he wants to." You love Lee Morgan (mainstream) and Lester Bowie — (not to be confused with David or Jim) — (avant).

Drums. At nineteen, with Miles in a quintet that included Wayne Shorter, Herbie Hancock, and Ron Carter, Tony Williams "took the drums somewhere else" — refuse to specify where. Jack deJohnette is a "black fire on the otherwise cold, white ECM label of jazz chamber music." You love Max Roach, Elvin Jones (former 'Trane sideman), Airto (mostly as a sideman), and Peter Erskine *(Weather Report)*. And like Sara Lee, nobody doesn't like Steve Gadd. Philip Wilson is the avant, and you get extra points for knowing that he played the blues with Paul Butterfield (or maybe you get them for not knowing).

Guitar. "Charlie Christian invented jazz guitar at eighteen, died at twenty-four, and has rarely been equaled to this day. Wes Montgomery — mainstream jazz guitar died with him — actually about four or five albums before he did, when he started recording for Creed Taylor." And, yes, folks — at one time George Benson was a jazz guitar player, and "he coulda been a contender," but if he prefers "merely to be a millionaire, that's his business."

Remember, you don't have to know the names of any of these artists' records, because you "don't buy jazz records — it's a live medium by nature, don't you think?" You hate, or better still, have never heard of Chuck Mangione, Tom Scott, John Klemmer, Ronnie Laws, Grover Washington, Buddy Rich (isn't he a comedian?), and Bob James.

If you still get in trouble, just maintain that "the white supremacist capitalist imperialist power structure" would never record any of the artists you like anyway!

The World of Opera

... voicing your expertise

Opera used to be blissfully easy to ignore, but since the invention of Beverly Sills and Luciano Pavarotti, it has become an issue. The Public Broadcasting System has added to the problem. With the flick of the wrist one can turn the tv dial from the relative solidity of *Laverne and Shirley* and find all manners and combinations of singers on a stage. Some are in lavish costumes, some are in evening clothes standing in front of the orchestra, most are singing in foreign languages, all are radiating the desire to be understood. Of course, they cannot be, and that is why the subtitle was invented — for the poor few who do not speak Italian, French, and German.

It is sad, but opera has become so accessible that it is getting harder and harder to admit that you know nothing about it. And so this primer for the ill informed is designed to help you keep your head at least above water with a real aficionado (who won't let you talk much, anyway) and to dazzle the billions of people who think that opera is only for the very rich. They, by the way, are right.

General Information

- Italian opera has beautiful melodies.
- German opera is long and "heavy."
- French opera has ballets and choruses.
- Russian opera is *Boris Godunov.*
- British opera is by Benjamin Britten, is in English, and the words are indecipherable.
- American opera is not an issue — sneer at the suggestion.

- And then there is Mozart.

A Word or Two About Mozart

- He wrote his first opera when he was twelve. It is called *La Finta Semplice*, is short and uninteresting, "but isn't it amazing that a twelve-year-old could write an opera?"
- *Don Giovanni* is the greatest opera ever written, but *The Magic Flute* (referred to only as "Flute" by Those In The Know) has the most glorious music.
- *The Marriage of Figaro* is delightful, and it is okay to prefer it in English. This is because "so much of the wonderful humor is lost in Italian." This is the only opera you will not prefer in the original language.

Wagner and His Problems

- He was a rotten human being.
- He married Franz Liszt's daughter, and he cheated on her.
- He wrote the words and the music to his operas.
- The *Ring* cycle is sixteen hours long and is too much for you. But you love *Tristan and Isolde.* It has sensual music.
- He was Hitler's favorite composer.

Verdi and Puccini

- Verdi is greater, but Puccini is "moving and realistic."
- Verdi wrote in three basic periods — early, middle, and late. (We're not kidding; this is real opera terminology.)
- Verdi wrote *Otello* when he was seventy-three, *Falstaff* when he was seventy-nine. They are up there with *Don Giovanni* for greatness.
- Puccini died before he finished *Turandot*. Someone else finished it.

Other Composers—A Roundup

- Rossini retired at thirty-seven and threw parties in Paris.
- Bellini died at thirty-three and wrote operas that are hard to sing.
- Donizetti contracted syphilis and wrote very little after he was thirty-five. He did, however, manage to squeeze in almost seventy operas.
- Mascagni never wrote anything as good as *Cavalleria Rusticana.*

This is enough knowledge for anyone. If you pass the following test, you are ready to buck even the most headstrong buff. Match the pairs. Answers appear nowhere in this volume. Good luck!

1. Hansel	A. letto
2. La	B. Callas
3. Arturo	C. Traviata
4. Rigo	D. Gretel
5. Maria	E. Toscanini

Now, if you can keep cracks about fat sopranos and stupid stories to yourself, you'll be in fine voice. Happy listening.

4

That's Entertainment

Hollywood I ══════

. . . I'm writing a screenplay, aren't you?

Hey, these days every other short-order cook from Astoria to Anchorage is working on a "treatment of the concept of an idea." After all, bulling your way into pictures is as old as the MGM lion. Many of the pioneer moviemakers who are now having reverential Bible-length tomes written about them started out as furriers, meat merchants, and shoe salesmen. And having a BFA in "cinemah" doesn't mean doo-doo to a modern mogul. You'll find that Faking cinematic savvy is basically a cinch, once you master some simple concepts and vocabulary. Here's what you need to know.

Movies are made by directors. In the old days they wore berets, ran around yelling "Cut!" through megaphones and didn't excite much attention off the set. But now, any director worth his celluloid drives a Mercedes Benz and has lots of people running around him including the paparazzi. In Filmdom today, the director is *it*. He is the Artist, and the movie is His Work. Speak of him as an *auteur* (AW-ter) who "writes" the movie with his camera, like a novelist with pen or a painter with brush. That's what some loony French eggheads suggested back in the fifties (among them François Truffaut and Jean-Luc Godard, two good names to throw around).

Today, there are college curriculums devoted to scrutinizing everything from *Gone With the Wind* to Bugs Bunny cartoons for Hidden Significance, because directors have a Vision, they have Something to Say. (Legendary producer Sam Goldwyn, who once barked, "You want to send a message? Go to Western Union!" is probably spinning in his grave.) So, never refer to a film by its stars or subject matter. Don't talk about "that boxing movie with Robert De Niro — it's Scorcese's *Raging Bull* and it's "about" machismo, violence, and the American Dream. *Some Like It Hot* isn't a Marilyn Monroe comedy: it's director "Billy Wilder at the peak of his career." In fact, it's très chic to avoid discussing the *content* of a movie entirely. Just tell gossip about and/or psychoanalyze the film's director. You don't actually have to have *seen* Woody Allen's new movie to authoritatively dismiss it: "Allen's such a neurotic narcissist. He's just been repeating himself since *Annie Hall*, and he hasn't really been funny since he split up with Diane."

It helps to be passionate about your favorites and least-favorites, cool about the in-betweens. You *love* Bertolucci. You *hate* Spielberg. You *understand* Bergman, but he leaves you cold. Be careful with pronunciations, and try to get acquainted with the proper nomenclature. For example, never speak of Federico Fellini or Francis Ford Coppola. It's Fellini and Coppola. (Conversely, mention actors and actresses, that inferior breed, by first names and nicknames, i.e., Kate Hepburn, Bob Redford, and Larry Olivier.) Skimming Pauline Kael in *The New Yorker* or Andrew Sarris in *The Village Voice* is good source material for this stuff, and also for the next important trick of the trade — strong cinematic vocabulary.

Again, talking about what actually goes on in a movie is for amateurs. You're concerned with camera work, cutting, the script, lighting, production values, the soundtrack. It's best to approach any popular movie from an oblique angle. In discussing, say, *Raiders of the Lost Ark*, mention "the imaginative set design. The script is weak," but the picture is "saved by some virtuoso editing" and "flashy production values."

Photography (that's "cinematography" to you) in general, and lighting and color in specific are safe subjects for inspiring respect in casual conversation. Besides the cognoscenti, who the hell ever notices the lighting in a flick unless it's so bad you can't see anything on the screen? To say you admire the "low-key lighting" in *The Godfather* is cool; to talk about the "musky, Vermeer-like interiors" in *Last Tango* is superhip, implying as it does that you were taking in more than Maria

Schneider's boobs and Brando's behind when you saw the picture.

Calling attention to the scoring is also smart (who listens?), and you'll get extra points if you can think of something bright to say about the sound mix, i.e., "The mix in the second-edition *Close Encounters* is vastly superior to the first." The ultimate in finesse is a reference to the print of the film itself, and that can actually give you a quick exit if you're being pinned on a movie you should have seen but didn't: "*Apocalypse Now?* Well, the print I saw was so poor I had to walk out on it."

Within the world of film buffery there are lots of more specific stances one can take. Here are two popular ones:

The Serious Cineaste. This is extremely heady turf, consisting of a kind of radical intellectualism — Film As Art — the hallowed ground where the elite meet. You read *Cahiers du Cinema* (preferably in the original French), *Sight and Sound*, and *Artforum*. Your idea of "fun" is watching creaky D.W. Griffith silent films and analyzing their "subtext." Watching super-8 movies consisting of close-ups of blank walls for an hour is a religious experience. You talk in terms of "semiology," "structuralism," and "pyrotechnics," as in: "The moving-camera pyrotechnics of Jerry Lewis betrays a mise-en-scéne that is subtextually tragic."

When serious cineastes talk to each other, they often don't even understand *themselves*, let alone the other person. But the more obscure your lingo, the deeper you appear to be. This is where real panache pays off. The advantage of this position is its great freedom of invention (there really *does* exist a movie called *Film Whose Surface Reaches The Clarity of Butter*, so wing it!). If pressed for a clear opinion, the kind of line that's unassailable is: "The only truly contemporary cinema is coming out of Poland."

The Popcorn Critic. This is the turf of the trendy, fashionable, fun-loving filmgoer. "I just caught *Eyeball Suckers From Mars* on a double bill with *Revenge of the Demon Nun* — you gotta see them on Forty-second Street because all the good stuff'll get cut out when it comes downtown! *Nun* has a Waring blender scene that makes *Texas Chainsaw Massacre* look like *Bambi!"* The basic drift here is the Bad-Is-Good (and Awful-Is-Great) syndrome. You revere and revel in pure trash, precisely because it has no pretensions to art or any significance at all.

This is the province of the cultist, the Midnight Moviegoer. Just pick a niche and carve it out, with the accent on visceral excitement, anything truly cheesy (from horrifically dubbed Japanese sci-fi to monumentally tasteless soft-core stuff (the films of Russ Meyer, i.e., *Beyond the Valley of the Dolls*) is fair game. You can take a stand for Annette Funicello as the greatest actress in Hollywood's history, say that "Clint Eastwood *is* cinema," boast of having seen *Night of the Living Dead* eight times or proclaim director John Waters *(Pink Flamingos, Polyester)* a genius. Cheap thrills is your meat, and your conversational zapgun is aimed at anything "serious," i.e., *Ordinary People.* "How boring can you get?" or "Meryl Streep puts me to sleep!" To pose as any kind of film buff, use these key words that are ambiguous enough to suggest You Know Something: "overrated" and "underrated," i.e., Brian De Palma is overrated (because he's just imitating Hitchcock); Brian De Palma is underrated (because he's *transcending* Hitchcock). "Classic," i.e., *Shaft's Big Score*, is a "classic of its kind." Adjectives, yea: "powerful," "major," and "important"; adjectives, nay: "thin," "minor," and "irrelevant." The granddaddy of them all is "cinematic." Saying a movie is "cinematic" is like saying the sky is "bluish." But it sure sounds PG (pretty good), doesn't it?

Hollywood II ═══════════

...films you haven't seen, directors whose names you haven't heard

*W*orking under the theory that the only thing worse than sitting through most foreign films is the inability to talk about them with authority, this chapter is designed to cut all conversations with tedious "film enthusiasts" short. The word, by the way, is *film;* movies are *Mary Poppins* and James Bond thrillers. Films are normally in other languages, with subtitles (a dubbed soundtrack "distorts the director's meaning") or directed by Orson Welles. There are some things you have to know about American-made works, and they are summarized at the end of the section.

- Jean-Luc Godard's politics get in the way of his filmmaking. *Breathless* (1960) showed great promise, but by *Weekend* (1967), which is the film with the huge traffic jam in it (all you have to know), he had become boring and preachy. He still is.
- Federico Fellini was a cartoonist before he became a director. (This is a little known fact that will get you high points.) He is very fashionable but goes to excesses, witness *Satyricon* (1967), a grotesque epic about ancient Rome. *8½* (1963) was a lavish, nearly incomprehensible work about a film director (guess who) with enormous self-doubt.
- Kurosawa is a great Japanese film director. His work is slow but beautiful to look at.
- Peter Sellers was funny, but Alec Guinness is the real "prince of English comics." Cite an early film, *Kind Hearts*

and Coronets (1949), in which he played eight roles, as evidence. In addition, he has greater "scope" than Sellers, whatever that means.

- Everyone likes François Truffaut's work, especially *Jules Et Jim,* about two friends in a romantic triangle. You think he's wonderful, too, and actually like *Mississippi Mermaid* (1969), which starred Catherine Deneuve and Jean-Paul Belmondo. The critics hated it, it disappeared without a trace, and you'll be the only one who's seen it.

- Buñuel made his first film in 1928. He is still around and is into surrealism.

As a bridge to the United States, now, we can include the following:

- Hitchcock really was as great as we thought when we first saw his work. *Vertigo,* with Kim Novak, is his most unappreciated film. See it and talk about it endlessly.

- Milos Forman, the Czech director, has a great sense of the American Scene. He directed the uproariously funny *Taking Off,* with Buck Henry (and Carly Simon in a tiny role — good trivia, high points), and the acclaimed but box-office-failed *Hair. The Firemen's Ball* (1968) was his breakthrough comedy.

Should you be forced to deal with American films, the following information and esoterica will get you everywhere:

- Orson Welles was twenty-six when he wrote, directed, and starred in *Citizen Kane.* It is a masterpiece. His next film, *The Magnificent Ambersons,* is beautiful to look at but is very boring. He is from Wisconsin, was once married to Rita Hayworth, and is currently very fat and doing voice-overs. He is to thought what Marlon Brando is to action.

- Do not dismiss Tuesday Weld as an actress simply because she looks like Sandra Dee. She proved herself in

The Cincinnati Kid and *Pretty Poison.* She "hasn't been given enough good roles."

- *Fantasia* (1940) by Walt Disney (and despite that) is a great film. In the '60s and '70s teenagers discovered it was fun to watch it stoned. Leopold Stokowski conducts a variety of classical music while cartoon characters prance about.
- It is okay to like late '30s and '40s American films, especially if Humphrey Bogart was in them. They are living proof that films aren't being made like they used to be.

You will, of course, continue to look down your nose at films that have been enormous box-office successes (except for *The Godfather*) as "good entertainment, but hardly in the same class with _____." Stick to the hard facts above and don't allow the other party to talk too much — all you really have to do is mention a little-known film by a well-known director and the conversation is all yours. Trivia is really big in this package — use it. And when confronted with a film or director totally unheard of, merely change the subject to Orson Welles. *Everyone* has a theory about him.

Books

. . . notes for the bestselling between-the-covers bibliophile

*I*n so many areas faking it can be chancy. You fake it in skiing. But suppose you find yourself in $500 Fiberglass boots with Heads strapped to them? You fake it in sailing. But suppose the breeze turns to a gale and you're told, "Take over!" You fake it in twin-engined, corporation jets and you're 30,000 feet up with thunderheads building and the pilot turns to you and says ...

But faking it in books is so SAFE. Furthermore, there is no such thing as a bibliophile who is *not* making use of his or her panache. At least to *some* degree. So here you are, right where you belong. And just think, there's literally *no* chance of your doing yourself bodily harm. So let's get right to it.

On the first level, which we will pass over quickly, you subscribe to *Book Digest*, which means just what it says. God knows, not chic and also not much fun. The next step is

reviews, of course, but be careful *which* reviews. *New York Times Book Review* and the *New York Review of Books.* The *Guardian* and *London Sunday Times.* And pretty much in that order.

Most people find it just too difficult to keep the title, author, publisher, subject, name of the reviewer, and the exact paper in which the review appeared all tied together, so don't bother. Just master a few basics and let the others muddle through the verities.

First off, you have a "field." It can be any one of the following:

- James Joyce
- Faulkner
- Dostoievsky in the original.

As for specific titles to be dropped into the conversation, confine yourself to *Gravity's Rainbow* (the most totally unread bestseller of all times) and *October Light.* Both books were extensively reviewed, "seriously," and anyone in a present-day discussion of books will have heard of them. But will of course *not* have read them.

You introduce either one when someone is holding forth on the delights or horrors of a current book, a perfectly accessible book such as Irwin's Shaw's *Bread* or John Irving's *Garp.* (Anyone who uses the full title of either book, i.e., *Bread Upon the Waters* or *The World According to Garp*, has at once revealed a lack of book expertise that should permit you to move right in, shouldering the unfortunate aside.)

"Shaw has probably peaked with *Bread . . .*" Or "Damn it all, Irving really *Believes* in Uncle Toad, and so do I!" Follow up with, "In *Gravity's Rainbow*, Pynchon was trying to work his way through much the same concept. And I think succeeded to far greater a degree than Shaw (Irving).

Or, "If Shaw (Irving) had bothered to read John Gardner's *October Light*, he would probably never have written *Bread (Garp)*."

Either statement will clearly establish your lead and should pretty well sweep the decks, permitting you to guide the conversation back to your own "field."

Once you're free to hold forth on your own choice, rapt attention is almost certainly guaranteed. Take the ball and run.

"James Joyce, an interesting prose experimentalist. Interesting, but failed. At least in my opinion."

Or, "But isn't *Finnegan's Wake* a distillation of a universal psyche? I've always thought of it as such."

Or, "So few people understand that Faulkner was *both* 100 years too soon and 200 years too late."

Or, "In translation Dostoievsky loses luminescence only to gain tendentiousness."

Joyce is not read, much less understood, by more than a dozen Irishmen (all of whom reside in Dublin) and six Americans (none of whom venture "off campus").

Faulkner is read, at least a chapter or two, by plenty of people, but find me one who's persisted from *Intruder in the Dust* straight through *Wild Palms.* Except you.

As for Dostoievsky, he's too apt to be confused with someone over at the UN or one of Catherine the Great's early lovers.

About any of the above, or in fact about any book that is mentioned about which you know nothing, you're pretty safe in dropping into a convenient pool of silence, or one of the following:

"All that discursive fecundity. Some people like it, I know. I just don't happen to be among them."

Or, "Too many ellipses there for my taste."

Or, "Fine, if you like to collect a lot of sodden profundities."

Or, "Along those same lines, how would you compare, say, *Naked Lunch* and *Bellefleur?*"

Of course, the oldest ploy in the world is reading the reviews and expounding from there. Nor is it a technique to be sneered at. In fact, a good meaty review should be able to save you the trouble of reading anything, much less *buying* it.

To fake it in the world of contemporary lit you should acquire:

- a complete set of Proust, in paperback only
- a two-volume set of the *OED (Oxford English Dictionary)* with the slipcase discarded and both the front and back covers partially shredded
- a few mangy-looking selections by Kafka, Samuel Beckett, Evelyn Waugh, Gide (of course), Nabokov, and William H. Auden
- a mothy shetland sweater with elbows out
- a twenty-four-inch-high stack of yellowed, back-dated *NYRB*s
- Half a dozen mugs with dried coffee rings inside them
- a handwoven Tibetan prayer rug
- a bottle of *good* vodka frozen inside a block of ice
- a handful of invitations from the Atheneum in Boston, all of them marked REGRET in an insouciant scrawl

Get rid of:

- Harold Robbins
- Jacqueline Susann and Judith Krantz (they're interchangeable)
- whatever dictionary you used in college
- all issues of *Time, Newsweek, Life,* and *National Geographic*
- Sidney Sheldon
- all your six-packs
- the tropical fish
- framed posters from the Museum of Modern Art
- the ceramic burro with the philodendron in its side baskets
- your bowling shoes

To be ill mannered in the world of the bibliophile is not only okay, it's a highly desirable trait. People who are high on books invariably have either wretched manners or no manners at all. Telephone calls are never terminated with "Well, goodbye," "See you then" or "Bye now." Rather, you just hang up, preferably catching the other party in midsyllable.

All shoes should be scruffy and unevenly worn down on the heels. Trousers bag, dress hems droop, and the bottom of purses and pockets *must* be strewn with tobacco, loose Lifesavers, and pens minus their caps. Suspenders are good, belts (except for a length of clothes line) are bad, anything that can clearly be defined as washable (such as shirts, khakis, skirts, T-shirts) should be avoided and replaced with dark woolens, such as those found in the bazaars of Eastern Europe.

Food is usually sparse. Bread is in hard, stale chunks and *never* sliced. Cheese is in dried-out hunks, no spreads, please! Fruit is all right as long as it's brown and soft to the touch.

Ailments should be confined to deep hacking coughs but never shin splints or slipped discs. Hives is all right, but poison ivy is not. Excessive sunburn is fine, but a smooth even tan is really bad.

Socks with holes or better still no socks.

Eyeglasses with a paperclip holding the hinge together.

No contact lenses, *please*!

Finally, don't hide your overdue bills. Pile them up in plain sight, topping the heap with a book of poems by Snodgrass.

And if you entertain in the evening, do it by candlelight and casually mention that the utility company has cut you off. Just remember to pull the main switch before the first guest arrives.

Legitimate Theater ══════

... playing the part of stage buff with panache

The theater is not *dead*, but alive and expensive. The neat thing about affecting expertise in this field is that it gives you a touch of class, even a dash of romance. To be "in theater" is to be involved in something serious; if you're not specifically an actor, playwright, director, or producer but you know something about the field — well, you must be some kind of Sensitive Guy or Gal. To play the part really well, you should familiarize yourself with some important names and a bit of behind-the-scenes terminology.

Acting To say an actor or actress is bad or good is much too simplistic. The classic *in*word here is *choices*. A good actor makes good or interesting choices, i.e., imaginative decisions on how to approach a role and/or piece of action. Pull a gun on a bad actor in a scene and he may spring back in horror, hands in the air. Pull a gun on Al Pacino and he'll more likely hold his ground, nod his head, and give you a strange little smile. That's a *good choice*, implying that there's something going on behind those intense little eyes of his. *Believability* is a high accolade. You "really believed [so-and-so] in that role," but you "didn't believe a single thing [so-and-so] did." Worse, "his technique was showing." Worse still, the crime of overacting: "She was chewing the scenery." The new word for *ham* is *cartoon*. A bad actor "plays it safe," whereas a good actor "takes risks." A fairly noncommittal, vaguely positive thing to say about an actor is that he "has good energy and brings a lot of life to his work." That kind of talk is especially effective if you've never seen or heard of the actor in question.

Playwrights The current Golden Boy of the American theater is Sam Shepard. Especially respected because he's a fine actor as well as a brilliant writer (and a handsome dude), he should be spoken of with reverence. He has "the most authentically American voice since Eugene O'Neill, his play *Tooth of Crime* was light years ahead of its time," and (superhip) "seeing the original production of *Cowboy Mouth* was the most exciting theatrical experience" you ever had.

Other popular but serious playwrights are David Mamet ("great ear for dialogue"), John Guare ("marvelously surrealistic"), Lanford Wilson ("wonderfully succinct") and Athol Fugard ("important"). In speaking of the more mainstream writers, it's cool to be grudgingly appreciative, i.e., "Neil Simon is actually underrated. That kind of stuff is harder to pull off than you'd think."

Of the established, you like Clifford Odets, Arthur Miller, Edward Albee. Tennessee Williams is God, but "he's lost it, of course." Sidestep the argument that serious theater is in trouble by saying, "There are a few good playwrights, so there'll always be a few good plays."

Directors and producers Harold Prince is a genius. Michael Bennett is a genius. Mike Nichols is a genius. In fact, legitimate theater is so costly to produce that anyone who manages to get more than one show on the boards is almost immediately ranked with Einstein. A hip approach to talking about these guys is to introduce some personal element in your assessment.

For example:

- Joseph Papp (Joe Papp to you) "has a lot of courage to try out so many things. I like the man, personally, but he's got bad taste."
- "David Merrick is a bastard — but he's a genius."

General guidelines Don't knock musicals. They've "kept Broadway alive for decades. If half the actors who put down musicals could sing and dance, they'd be in them." Stephen Sondheim is a genius, Bob Fosse is a genius — even though he's Gone Hollywood. Apropos Hollywood, the elitist, pro-New York stance goes: "Film acting isn't *acting*. The camera does everything for you. Good actors always return to the theater because it stretches them more."

In talking of off and off-off Broadway, the party line is: "Sure there's great stuff going on downtown. But you have to wade through so much crap to find it!" Of shows that move from off to on Broadway: "The play worked so much better in an intimate setting." Critics are the scum of the earth, but you do respect their power; reviews can nurture a struggling show to a longer run or kill it in its tracks. On the other hand, the public sometimes proves critics wrong. Generally speaking, "Bad shows close, good shows stay open." However, sometimes a "milestone in theatrical history" fails miserably at the box office. Your defense? "The public couldn't handle it."

A final tip: Nothing sounds better (and means so little) than the old double whammy — so-and-so is "a director's director" or "an actor's actor." You can mix and match ("an actor's director") ad absurdum. Try saying this stuff with a straight face. And panache!

5
Getting There/ Being There

Resorts

. . . the latest and greatest bastions of escape

*T*he good news is that the world is opening up — spas in Tibet, condos on the Black Sea, casinos in Swaziland — which means that you can almost always drop a resort name guaranteed to be unvisited by anyone present. The bad news is that with rising unemployment, more and more people are lolling on faraway beaches, gazing up into the exotic foliage of unnamed trees or drifting down waters uncharted on any *Mobil Guide* map.

Faking it in the resort-visiting world divides roughly into two categories: the tried 'n' true (but exclusive, of course) and the never-even-heard-of-it before.

In the first category, year in, year out, nothing beats Cap d'Antibes and Palm Beach. Shahs, princes, and ex-presidents have spent literally millions trying to displace both. They've all failed. Sure, there are good seasons and some not-so-good seasons, but by and large, the Cap and Palm are staples, names to be dropped right off in the warm-up rounds before you settle into lesser-known stuff.

Visiting regularly is good. Having a villa (not a cottage, please) is better. Of course your own yacht affords a pleasing mobility not to be sneered at. If you have your own villa but are not in it at the moment it's because you've lent it to close friends who needed anonymity. In one breath, this establishes your largesse and your coterie of high-born intimates.

In the days of the great ships snobbery was affected by means of luggage labels — six-inch-long things labeled CUNARD or WHITE STAR and backed with forever glue. These are now of course passé, and leaving the three initial luggage tags on your stuff is all too apt to result in your gear being shipped to DFW while you await it in SYD. Plus:

- You don't jet, you "Concorde."
- You *never* take cruises, although you *do* cruise.
- You simply *have* to be out of town over Christmas and the New Year.
- You wouldn't know a house trailer if one were parked in your front yard.
- You can't remember where you got your hand-carved walking stick. It could have been Nairobi, but it could also have been Bombay.

Where do you stay in ...

- London? A little place near Princess Gate (with a wink).
- Paris? With a friend. Toujours (ha ha).
- Rome? Have you ever seen the private apartments in the Vatican?
- Athens? I was willed a sixteenth-century villa half an hour outside the city. Ten years ago, if you'd asked me I'd have *given* it to you. Now, of course, I'm glad I was too busy to get rid of it.
- Peking? In the French Embassy.
- Moscow? In the Cuban Embassy.
- Tokyo? My company keeps a little ...

Tastes in resorts are fickle. Nassau used to be *it*, now we leave it to show biz and the Mob.

Once upon a time Biarritz was overbooked and turning away the swells by the gross. Today it rains a lot and only Europe's blue-blooded bleeders are in summer residence.

Aspen was good until it went artsy; Puerto Vallerta was great until the iguana was imported. Mt. Tremblant was fantastic until the chef died and it also became possible to jet off to the Alps.

Now Cozumel, Mahe, Malindi, and Agadir are nosing into the front ranks and, until further notice, may be mentioned at will. The Great Barrier Reef is one of those perennials, as is the middle fork of the Salmon River. Alaska, so vast and unvisited, makes great name dropping. Any Eskimo-like word — Achoo, Tootoo, Meetu — will serve as one of those uncharted little islands where "we went to film the Kodiaks." You were flown in. Incredible scenery. "In fact, if you'd like to see my slides. . . ."

Safari in Africa, once the epitome of Teddy Roosevelt-like chic, is now almost humdrum. Buses from the lodge to the feeding pride of lions depart on schedule. If your camera jammed, buy yourself a complete set of African wildlife slides as you depart Nairobi Airport.

Canoe trips up the Amazon, if it's far enough up, are acceptable and even enviable. Just be certain it's piranha season (they're harmless as minnows fifty weeks a year) and that missionaries were sacrificed there less than two years before.

Even the fabled Roof of the World — Bhutan, Sikkim, and Tibet — are being turned into revolving doors for the Nikon-bedecked tourist. But if you can allow that you stayed "at the palace" (lowercase *p*), it might just be worth a brief mention.

Wherever you go, you're expected to *do* something. Lying around on a deck chair or on a beach might have been fine a few years ago, but no more. Vacations must be verb packed. You:

- salmon fish
- "go" for marlin
- hit the boards (ski)
- try your luck (roulette)
- trek into the interior
- raft downstream
- get some fantastic gorilla close-ups
- crew
- scuba

You *never:*

- deep-sea fish
- go to ski school
- gamble
- take a camping trip
- get on this tippy platform kind of thing
- have the s--- scared out of you by these apes
- throw up
- pay ten bucks to go down this ladder on the side of a reef

On Being a Texan

... oiling your image

*T*he advantages of being mistaken for a Texan (born and bred) increase in direct proportion to the distance that exists between you and the Lone Star State. In Oklahoma or Arkansas, for instance, to be a Texan is no advantage. It might even earn you a crinkled fender or a long wait at the bar. Texans are considered pushy by their near neighbors for no reason other than that they are. Pushy. But if you allow that you are a Texan in, say, Anchorage, Tokyo, Moscow, or even New York, you'd be surprised at the effect it has.

- You've no need to prove you're solvent. Isn't every Texan? Oil wells and heads of cattle never have to be translated into a bottom line of dollars and cents.

- Your credit is good, no problem.
- Your social worth is very apt to nip sharply upward. After all, who knows when the mood will strike to charter yourself a 707, fill it with all your friends and just fly them all down to the ranch for a week of round-up, ribs, dust-kicking, and square dancing?

Since Texas is incredibly hot, incredibly humid, very dusty, and chockablock full-up with Texans, you should consider yourself very fortunate you'll be able to pass yourself off as a Texan without ever having to go near the place. Let's assume that you're going to a party where you won't know a soul. This is a perfect setup for you.

Dress with care. Summer or winter — it makes no difference. Your wardrobe is the same. (It's always summer in Texas, isn't it?) Wear a shirt devoid of ordinary buttons but covered with pearl snap fasteners. Your nondesigner jeans are snugged into place with a three-inch-wide belt fastened with a great, big, silver hand-worked buckle. A bandana goes round your neck, unless you have one of those itty-bitty bolo ties fastened with a turquoise clip. Boots, of course — pull-ons with undershot heels and pointy toes. All jewelry is silver or turquoise, and you're free to wear as much of it as you like. Top off the whole outfit with plenty of leather fringe.

Address your hostess, at least at first, as "Ma-am?" and everyone else as "Honey."

Under no circumstances introduce the subject of your home state. You'll be surprised how quickly it will be brought up. When it is, just hang your head a little, smile and allow that, as a matter of fact, "ah doo come from Taix-iss."

At the bar, ask very politely if "bah enny chance yall carry Lone Star or Pearl bee-ah?" and then feel free to drink whatever you usually drink.

If you're in a restaurant, ask the waiter if "bah enny chance yall carry chicken frahd steak?" and then feel free to order whatever you usually eat.

Being from Texas permits you plenty of conversational latitude. You can discuss anything at all having to do with LBJ ... the ranch, the Pedernales (usually dried up), the herd, the Lil Lady he left behind and, of course, KTBC and the Texas Broadcasting Company — all part and parcel of the LBJ spread.

You can quote Uncle Sam, and you don't mean the whiskery

guy on the recruiting posters but rather the late Sam Rayburn, now gaveling things to order in the Big House in the Sky.

Your favorite authors are Tom Lea, Larry King, and Willie Morris . . . "not that ah read all that much."

No problem about your schooling. There was and is only one place to go and that's the University of Texas. Be sure you get it just that way; talking about "Texas University" is a sure giveaway.

Your politics are simple enough. You're against the Godless Communists ("ah don't keer WHERE they are"), you're "jest as sure as ahm sitting hyar that John Connally was framed by those Yankee dairy farmers, since he'd niver tech a penny that didn't belong to him fair and square."

Your religion is Baptist and you can still spin some pretty fine yarns about the day your folks took you down to the river when the preacher was having a big mass baptisin' and you had to wade right in ("hold mah nose, lay back down and let the love of Jesus wash all over me").

You bank at Texas Commerce and you have "plenty of money ridin' on the Dallas Cowboys this year". . . you and Clint Murchison, Jr., who's probably, next to yer Daddy, the best friend you have in the whole gosh-dern world.

If the strolling troubadours come over to your table, make sure you ask for one of your three favorites: *Yellow Rose of Texas, Cotton Eyed Joe,* or *Tumblin' Tumbleweed. Deep in the Heart of Texas* is certainly a longtime favorite, but you don't often ask for it in restaurants or bars because it's too apt to overturn glasses, what with that hand-clapping and all.

If you find the role of being Texan sufficiently appealing to want to continue the posture on your own premises, you've only to make a few minor changes in your digs to have the effect be not only persuasive but also charming.

Hang a couple of prong horns over your front door and use them as a rack for umbrellas. If you have any kind of shotgun or rifle, that would be even better. Scatter throw pillows embroidered with LONE STAR STATE on your sofa, and wherever you can — on stationery, on your mailbox, up over your mantle, in the middle of your floor, on your dining room table — paint a big letter W with an extra tail added onto each end of it. This is the Running W, which is the brand mark for the King Ranch. Since the King Ranch belongs to a corporation in which there are a great many stockholders, why not join right in there with them? In case anyone wants to know about the ol' homestead, you can pass along (modestly) any of the following thous:

- 825 thou acres
- 60 thou head of cattle
- 2 thou miles of fence
- 3 thou oil wells

Macrame hangings made out of rope, bandanas sewn together as antimacassars, plenty of basketry, tattered copies of *Texas Monthly*, a pair of wooden stirrups nailed on a board and used as bookends for *Reader's Digest Condensed Books Omnibus* volumes, catalogues from Neiman Marcus and a summer-clearance flyer from Little's Boot Company in San Antonio should add to your validity.

If you can manage to find chairs and tables constructed out of branches of trees, all the knots and the bark still in place, by all means load up on them. When people comment, tell them it's all cottonwood and "off the spread." Keep a bottle of hoof dressing on the antelope-skin coffee table. Tucked under the bottle, in full view, is your invitation to the Crystal Charity Ball.

If you're out with friends and you have a chance to drive, remember to go too fast, especially within the city limits where it's more noticeable. If your speed is sufficiently outrageous, it may cause your friends to ask you to slow down, which will give you a chance to tell them that you don't believe in the double-nickle speed limit and that there's not a word of truth — and in fact it's just dirty Commie propaganda — to the rumor that we're running out of oil.

Keep your fridge full of Dr. Pepper. If you can find the little pasted papers and those tiny drawstring cotton sacks of tobacco, by all means roll your own, practicing until you manage the whole thing with one hand (you're used to keeping the other on the reins).

There's hardly any need to remind you that your favorite flower — no, your favorite posy — is the blue bonnet, for which you'll have to substitute either bachelor buttons or delphinium. But don't worry. Once you're more than a 100 miles from the nearest Texas state line, nobody will know the difference.

Keep your hat on your head by means of a cork under your chin. Don't let anyone in your presence badmouth the Hunt Brothers for trying to hog all the silver in the world — "yall jes doan understand, thas all" — and tell anyone who'll listen that "we'll every las one of us be long gone before anyone gets around to figuring out how to power an auto*m*obile by solar energy." And that's God's truth.

New York, New York ═══════

. . . sophisticated street smarts

There are few areas in the known world where being from New York does not place you at a distinct advantage. New York City is universally accepted as the fastest paced, most sophisticated, and exciting city extant. By New York, of course, we mean Manhattan. Despite the fact that the mention of Brooklyn can inspire a certain awed reaction in oriental countries, it rarely brings to mind the word *sophisticated*. The Bronx, Queens, and Staten Island exist, for our purposes, only in the minds of their residents.

New Yorkers may not always be loved, but they will always be respected. Mere survival in the urban jungle that is Manhattan is rated equally with thriving anywhere else. If you would like to bask in the warmth of this almost worshipful reverence but have never been nearer the "Big Apple" than Dubois, Pennsylvania, here are some banners you can wave.

East Side, West Side, all around the town . . . New York is divided into unofficial districts well known to the natives. You can pick your assumed point of origin to fit your own personality.

Upper East Side (according to lower Manhattanites, anything east of Fifth Avenue and north of Fourteenth Street). Upper East Siders are either young and upwardly mobile or older and already rich. They dress expensively but not necessarily well (even their jogging outfits are expensive, no cutoffs here). They *are* the establishment. If you are pretending to be from the UES, feel free to discuss futures and commodities and the long lines for movies on Friday nights (it never occurs to an Upper East Sider to go on a weeknight or, horrors, a weekday).

You have "no crime problem" but it costs you the "gross national product of a small country to park the car." You have "all the major museums within walking distance" but "never have time to go."

Men wear conservative suits for business and formal occasions; women wear furs as far into summer as they dare. Both favor the ubiquitous jogging outfits for everything else.

Upper West Side (above Fifty-ninth Street and west of "the Park" — Central, of course). The UWS is like a hipper version of the UES. It is establishment with artistic pretensions. Here reside successful artists, writers, actors, musicians, etc. They moved here for "the neighborhoody quality." Unfortunately, their affluent influx drove the property values up and the small shops (that gave it that "neighborhoody" quality) out.

As a West Sider manqué, you "love off off Broadway theater" and "attend viola da gamba concerts at the local church." You "bemoan dogs in Central Park" but "love the open-air Shakespeare." (For some reason, Upper East Siders, who are equally close to the park, never enter it, except sometimes to jog.)

Men wear tweed or corduroy suits and jackets with elbow patches, while women sport the high-fashion equivalent of earth shoes. Both Upper East Siders and Upper West Siders roller-skate.

Hell's Kitchen (Forty-second Street to Fifty-ninth Street west of Sixth Avenue). Being from Hell's Kitchen is only interesting if you were born there — no one nice moves there. If you can carry off a faintly menacing air and have a Mediterranean appearance that could pass for Hispanic or Italian, you may want to capitalize on the fear value of pretending to

be from this part of New York. When asked if it is "true that you can buy machine guns in the candy stores," reply, "Only if you are big enough to reach the counter."

Sleeveless undershirts are de rigeur for men, winter and summer. For women, it is sleeveless shifts (and shiftless husbands). Tattoos for both.

Chelsea (Fourteenth Street to Thirty-fourth Street west of Fifth Avenue). This is as close to the West Village as you should admit to living if you are not gay. People who live in Chelsea would like to live on the Upper West Side but cannot afford it.

West Village (Houston to Fourteenth Street west of Washington Square). The West Village is not a good banner to wave if you want to get the full benefit of the New York Mystique. West Villagers tend to be either gay or 1950s-style bohemians. New York gays are indistinguishable from gays anywhere else and are thus subject to the same treatment, for better or for worse. Outdated bohemians are merely fake Europeans and, as such, unlikely to impress the real thing.

SoHo (for "south of Houston" — that is pronounced "howston" — also known more esoterically as NoCal, for North of Canal). Claiming to be an artist from SoHo will give you away immediately as a fraud and a charlatan; everyone from New Jersey to New Guinea knows that all the artists have moved from SoHo to Hoboken. Claiming to be a lawyer with a million-dollar co-op loft will ring much truer. You have friends who "spend a minimum of $200 a week on cocaine" and "have never been kept waiting more than five minutes at Studio 54."

Lower East Side (formerly known as the East Village and before that as the Lower East Side — Houston to Fourteenth Street and the Bowery to Avenue D). You are in a new-wave band or know someone who is in a new-wave band, or, at the very least, you know someone who knows someone, etc. . . . You have no visible means of support and never appear in broad daylight (in this respect you resemble Dracula, also in skin tone). Male and female, you wear black pants and black leather jackets — winter and summer. Or, you may be old and Ukranian (if you are young and Ukranian you will have moved to Queens).

You now know all you need to know about New York City. And that, as any true New Yorker will tell you, is all you need to know.

6
Fields of Wonder

Architecture ═══════════

...finding your way in the world of sticks, stones, glass, and steel

F irst of all, before you can hope to act with panache in the company of architects, it's essential to recognize the Prime Fact that overshadows every other consideration in the life of any architect.

FRUSTRATION Pure. Unalleviated. Nonstop.

An architect, like the unicorn, is a creature of misconception. The function of someone who describes herself as a *Builder* is unquestioned. One rock atop another, and soon there's your little house on the prairie. Where was the architect?

Nowheresville.

An architect is haunted by the niggling suspicion that he may be unnecessary, and may, like an unpleasantly swollen aorta, simply be bypassed. In fact, very often *is* bypassed.

The pyramids, the Great Wall of China, the Roman catacombs, name me the architect.

See?

And yet to arrive at this nonstatus status, consider what's involved. Four years of college, three more in architectural school, a couple more as a gofer, and then what can the newly arrived architect expect to find? Unemployment, probably.

For a fortunate few, there's a long gray future consisting of a kitchen stool, a drawing board, a T square, and the chance— *if* the firm gets the contract — to design the profile of a girder that would be used to support the overhang of a lineoleum factory's warehouse. The lives of architects are slog-along existences, replete with groins and quoins, with pediments and plinths. Any hopes they might harbor of getting to design the National Saudi Arabian Petro High Rise or the Can-Am-Mex Natural Gas Friendship Palace are about as realistic as hoping that Queen Elizabeth will undergo a sex-change operation and take up life as a sumo wrestler.

Contrast this to the life of a med student: by the end of the first term, she is going all out with cadavers in the hospital basement. Second term finds her making Grand Rounds with Drs. Welby and Kildare. Third term she is hovering, scalpel in hand over an unsuspecting assortment of tonsils, adenoids, and other superflua. By the fourth term, the doctor-to-be is cheerfully lopping and slicing away, secure in the knowledge that the third-hand, rusted-out VW bug that spends all its time at the shop is very shortly to be metamorphosed into a gleaming Jag.

To boot, a medical student soon acquires the respected title of doctor, while the architect, the whole of his natural and unnatural life, will probably remain just Chuck or Mary Sue or Herb.

All of the above is herewith included as a plea for tolerance on your part as you slide into the choppy waters of the architects' social mainstream.

"Less is more," said Mies van Der Rohe (who is to architecture what Rin Tin Tin is to canine heroics), not knowing how squarely he was coming down on the head of the architect's tack.

Architects adore tossing words around in this quasi-meaningless style. They frequently speak of Honesty, Purity, Strength, Integrity, and Totality. They're not talking of religious conversions, of love affairs, or moral doctrine. They're talking about walls, floors, roofs, ceilings, and downspouts.

It is, as you can readily see, a far-out, loose-goose way of using language and is a style that you can easily imitate.

For every American architect, there is One God. Uncle Frank. You can love him. You can hate him. You just can't ignore him. If you decide you're pro-Frank Lloyd Wright, you're seriously concerned with the sincerity of Falling Water, the Price Tower, and Taliesin West.

- They *speak* to you.
- They represent an ineffable balancing of void and bulk.
- They represent certain essential syntactical nuances.
- They render obsolete all seminology of infrastructures.
  OR THEY DON'T. Either way is okay.

If you find yourself closeted with FLW freaks, no problem. Stretch your verbal wings and soar. But what if you've fallen in with the anti sorts, the cons, the nay sayers?

Still no problem. The anti-Frank Lloyd Wright school of architecture consists exclusively of a single, supersterile, highminded German: Walter Gropius. It was he who founded something called the Bauhaus (say, *bowhows*) school of architecture. It's fair to say that the Bauhaus was/is to architecture what Othello is to wife abuse.

- Wright hated Gropius.
- Gropius hated Wright.

It's up to you to choose one and conspicuously ignore the other. Since both Wright and Gropius are safely dead, you can feel free to interpret the work of either one more or less on your own terms, provided you confine yourself strictly to a vocabulary that is nonconcrete. Rather, keep it airy. Steer clear of facts. Avoid, for instance, hazarding a guess as to the height of any building, the purpose for which it was constructed, or even whether or not it still stands.

In architecture as in everything else, the best are dead. But just to be on the safe side, tuck into a small mental cranny the names of a few who still seem to be with us.

- There's I.M. Pei. He's in big with Jackie O., which assures him a certain highly paid visibility. Like the Kennedy Library on the Charles.

- There's Yamasaki. We can thank him for the World Trade Center, both towers. And just remember, in case the discussion turns really heavy, that it was Yamasaki who built a multimillion dollar disaster that the city fathers in their inestimable wisdom finally stuck sticks of dynamite under (all three blocks) and blew it right off the face of the St. Louis downtown map.

- There's John Portman. He designed the Regency Hyatt Hotels, but as a result of the law suits for the collapse of the two crosswalks in the Kansas City Regency Hyatt, you're probably better off not saying too much about him.

That should be enough to get you through even a longish evening in the company of architects. How do you dress? You can't go wrong if you arrive decked out in a porkpie hat, a flowing cravat, and an opera cape. It's a get-up that will immediately identify you as being conversant with the Frank Lloyd Wright style, and then, depending on how the winds of public opinion blow, you can let it be known that you dress this way either because you admire the Great Man or because you think he was a Silly Ass, a viewpoint that you're only out to emphasize with these ridiculous-looking clothes.

High Finance ===============

. . . snaking your way to the bottom line

*O*nce upon a time, not very long ago either, the average three-piece-suited wage earner salted a little bit away in the neighborhood savings and loan every payday. He carried a sober-looking dark green or navy blue passbook in which was recorded his steady 5 percent interest. At this same S&L he negotiated his thirty-year home mortgage at the scandalously high interest rate of 6.5 percent, and, once in a blue moon, if he lucked into an extra grand or two, courtesy of the demise of an elderly maiden aunt, he took a flyer in the blue chips with AT&T. His broker was happy.

Today, such a creature is as extinct as the hairy mammoth. His contemporary counterpart has one, two, and maybe three different Dreyfus Liquid Assets Fund accounts. He takes full advantage of the fund's instant-liquidity factor by drawing down at will to pick up an interest in the next hot little Silicone Valley offering or perhaps to get in right on the ground floor (pouncing on a few hundred shares moments after the stock comes on the market) of the very latest in gene splitting and splicing. He talks with ease about taking back paper, balloon payments, and wraparound mortgages. His broker is miserable.

CONCLUSION: It's not as easy by half today to pass yourself off as a savvy sort in the field of stocks, bonds, commodity futures, and commercial paper as it once was. It's not as easy because chances are your nice little old cleaning lady with the rolled stockings and the hack ripple-sole working shoes with windows cut in the side to ease her bunions already knows as much about the niceties of handling money in today's roller coaster economy as did the 1970 senior partner in your local buttoned-down, sixteen-stroke-handicap, two-martini-lunch investment firm.

It's not as easy. Which is not at all to say that it's impossible.

Let's suppose for a moment that for reasons not worth exploring you are invited to a party that you know will be populated by individuals involved in High Finance. You could, of course, elect to attend the function, all eyes, ears, and grateful-for-anything-I-can-learn. It's an attitude that would by no means go unappreciated, particularly in a world where virtually everyone wants to hand out advice and no one ever wants to be thought of as a taker of same.

But why spread joy if with scarcely more effort you could spread envy, awe, and unrest? Why should you not have potential investors clinging worshipfully to even your most casual utterances?

Unlike the soap or vacuum cleaner business, the most important people in any investment firm are the salesmen. (No, the term will never be *salesperson* because, in theory, anyway, females don't really exist in the world of investment, except of course as stenos, gal Fridays, and switchboard jugglers. This mind-set will continue to prevail regardless of how many women move into executive suites. Such creatures will always and always be rara avis and in no way a threat to the all-male scene.)

Anyone insufficiently with it to hack the double-quick, two-step, charm-without-end role of a salesman, ends up in the back room working out the yield spread analysis on his Apple II. Sharing a phone.

So you're a salesman on Wall Street, eh?

Individual or institutional?

Don't be funny. I have some good friends who do the individual stuff, but don't ask me why. No, it's strictly institutional for me.

Don't make the mistake of taking seriously the hype dished out by Mad Ave and in so doing identify yourself as being with one of those banks where nest eggs are kept or one that depends on over-the-hill baseball players to inspire public confidence.

Absolutely not.

All banks, no matter how glossy their ads, how recherché their art collections, are notoriously unimaginative when it comes to making new bucks out of old.

"On Wall Street, eh? Any firm we ever heard of?"

"Oh . . . probably not. Not really."

Only when pressed does your full picture emerge. You and two other guys, a trio of smooth-cheeked geniuses, whose total ages don't add up to one hundred, all jog or cycle to your brand-new suite of offices at 14 Wall, where you're running a small sexy boutique with hot venture capital ideas. Twice

a week squash at the Downtown Athletic Club, lunch washed down with Perrier avec twist, and an in-house open line to Jedda, Paris, and London.

Dead as the Davy Crockett boom is the image of the cigar-smoking, brandy-drinking Daddy Warbucks in a mink shawl collar, a homburg, and a twice-a-year booking of the four-room master suite on the flagship of the Cunarders.

Where you're seen between nine and five is just as vital as the makeup of your portfolio, so early on you let it be known that you make it a habit to lunch every day at Le Vallauris on Beaver Street.

Upstairs?

Downstairs?

Be careful! It's downstairs; there is no upstairs.

If you're dialoguing with the bond people, you lunch at Harry's over on Hanover Square.

Upstairs?

Downstairs?

Strictly downstairs, and in this instance there *is* an upstairs, but you should never admit to being there since it belongs exclusively to the computer jocks from Stanford, polyester double knits from Wharton, and the quants from the U of Chicago.

If it's not bonds you have on your mind but stocks, then it's still Harry's where you lunch, *but* it's Harry's at the American Exchange over near the WTC (or, if you're from up-country, the World Trade Center).

Of course, you have occasion to entertain clients you prefer to keep not only under wraps but sheltered from the harsh winds of commercial eateries. Naturally, you opt for lunch in-house.

The all-oriental cuisine of AIG appeals to you; it's a pleasant change from the chef salad/thinly sliced filet routine.

The food at Salomon Brothers may not be that spectacular, but spectacular is exactly what you'd term the view from those floor-to-ceiling windows overlooking the harbor.

And for pure Old World charm, your vote goes to Lehman Brothers.

"When they moved their offices from 1 William over to 55 Water, they really went all out on the ambience. True, a lot of people object to it and think it's passé, but personally I think those marble floors and all that heavy old original brass is just great."

"As for that Nautilus equipment in the exec gym . . ."

All of the above is just as applicable to the female exec as it is to the male. Women are not authoritatively classified or defined. This is a fact that, if you are a woman, you should milk for all it's worth. You will quickly find out that when you announce at any kind of social gathering that you are "on the street," you will earn instant respect from everyone present who is smart enough not to take you for a hooker. It's too bad about your female wardrobe, but try not to mind too much. You are, after all, earning approximately 100 times the national average wage. Of course, they might have been tipped off by your clothes. One year all the women execs on the street were in navy blue chalk stripes. Beige took over the next year. Right now, too bad, it's loden green.

Much has been written about maintaining the feminine look in the boardroom, mostly through blouses with frilly jabots, but it's advice that's gone unheeded. Female sartorial chic on Wall Street has yet to achieve the minimal standards set by Ana Pauker of the Hungarian Commintern in the 1950s.

Because there are so few of you in the innermost councils of finance, you are excluded from a good many of the perks that your male counterpart takes for granted. For instance, no access to the brand-new company gym; or access only between 10:00 A.M. and noon, just when the lines are burning up with the closing prices in London, Paris, and Zurich.

Doesn't all this absurd male chauvinism annoy you? Not really. Actually it usually amuses you. Besides, "I don't have that much time to waste even thinking about it. My accounts keep me pretty busy, what with Concordeing over to London twice a month for conferences and, at the same time, trying to keep in touch with our offices in Paris, Rome, and Rio."

Do you see any chance of changes in the near future in this ridiculous sexism?

"*Well* . . . maybe."

"Really! Tell us why."

"Because over at . . . oops, better not name names, hmmm? So let's just say that one of the most prestigious firms on the street has just constructed an enormous bathroom suite on its top executive floor and, to date, the gender of the fixtures is one of the financial world's best-kept secrets. But if you promise not to breathe a word to a soul, I'll tell you that I know for a fact that they're installing floor-to-ceiling mirrors, there's to be a sit-down dressing table and all the fixtures are pink."

Horticulture

. . . the greening of your thumb

"**W**hy should I even bother to try to fake it into the earthy, fertile world of the green and the growing? For only a little more effort I could pass myself off as an astronaut, a reader of the Rosetta stone, or a polo player. There's no percentage in it. . . ."

Wrong.

The payoff for successfully faking it as a horticulturist—a person beloved for composting and mulching, for staking up and cutting back—is subtle but definite. Pass yourself off as a horticulturist, and at once you sprout an image that is as likable as it is useful.

If, for instance, you should overdraw your bank account, well, people think, there's really no great harm in that. No one would ever think of you as a chiseler, an embezzler, a juggler of the boss's books. Not a horticulturist. There is something about someone who grows veggies that just makes unthink-able any suggestion of serious wrongdoing.

Your moods and quirks—especially your quirks—will be indulged. You hate your neighbor? The lady who lives opposite you? The kid on the next block? Feel free to say so. Loving zinnias and rutabagas as you do, you're allowed to wallow in strong dislikes in other areas, and with as much verve as you'd like.

Feel free, as well, to let your car rust out, your clothes go out of style, and to be generally uninformed about the world around you. No one will criticize. Your world, it's generally conceded, is a rose-scented refuge visited by songbirds, lovers, and poets.

You begin with a pair of rubber-soled, supersensible shoes— L.L. Bean duck shoes are ideal, but any old pair of flat, ugly shoes will do. Get them well caked with good wet dirt (here- after known as *soil*), dry them carefully on a piece of news- paper, and, once the stuff is hard as iron, drop the shoes just behind your front door. Granted, this introduction to the haute monde of horticulture is more effective if you don't live in an apartment. But even if you *do* live in an apartment, follow through as instructed above. Even the most heartless of con- crete-and-steel cities have public parks and botanical gardens, both of which, as a horticulturist, you keep high on your most frequented list.

Save enough of this same soil to fill several flats (the gar- dener's term for poorly constructed oblong wooden boxes about three inches deep). Put the flat in plain view on your window sill and never mind that you have nothing growing in them. In those flats you are *starting* seeds.

"What kind of seeds?"

For this one you dip back into your high school Latin; just about anything you can manage to retrieve therefrom will do the trick.

"Mea culpa japonnicus."

"Ignobile vulgus alba."

Growing anything from seed rates head and shoulders over growing the same thing from seed*lings*. The difference of double fudge chocolate layer cake from scratch versus a box of Duncan Hines mix.

It's a good idea to lay a pane of clear window glass on top of the flats of soil. This barrier method prevents snoops from peering in too closely, and it prevents friends (ha-ha) from stubbing out their ciggie butts in the growing medium. A single butt sticking up out of your seed nursery is enough to undo a good deal of high-potency horticultural effects.

Seed catalogues are usually free. But not always. It pays off, however, to spend a few bucks in order to have a good fat collection of these four-colored, lavishly illustrated booklets. Stack them on chairs and tables in your living room.

"Just what are you thinking of ordering?"

Don't let that one worry you. You're sick and tired of what they have to offer, so this year you're having "just about everything" shipped in from a little nursery man you know over in the Cotswold country in England.

Having the cream of the crop of catalogues but choosing to bypass them is always a good shot.

Muddy shoes, boxes of only dirt, seed catalogues in ample evidence—that's a good start but certainly not enough. Somewhere along the line you're going to have to have a plant or two to substantiate your high rank in the horticultural hierarchy. For this we recommend the following. Acquire from your local supermarket—especially right after Christmas— one of those woebegone poinsettia plants. Failing that, get yourself a hard-nosed, stiff-limbed rubber plant. If that isn't totally indestructible, it's the next thing to it.

Take it home and lop off the branches on one side of it, right at its waistline. Now take one of those lopped-off branches, peel away any foliage. (You now have an unidentifiable plant.) Finally, take a foot or so of ordinary gauze bandage and *tie* the butchered-up limb back onto the waist of the parent plant.

Of course it looks funny. A plant with a bandaged middle. But it's exactly what you want.

"That 'bandaged plant' over there near the window? Oh, no, it's not *bandaged* at all; it's a graft I'm starting. The Department of Agriculture wanted to know if I could come up with a disease-resistant peach tree. That's just one of several I'm trying out for them."

If you're not really into the finer points of housekeeping, passing yourself off as a horticulturist is right up your alley. Raggedy, slightly soiled slipcovers, frayed-out rugs, tabletops with cigarette burns and glass rings all over them are all right in character. It's not the *house* you care about after all, it's the *garden.*

Now what if you have no garden?

That's because (sigh) you spend all your time running around as a consultant to other people who want to know if they should replace all their privet with hemlocks or whether to turn their artificial goldfish pond and waterfall into a Shakespearean herb garden.

As a horticulturist, you're free to wear the most disreputable clothes ... the raggedier, the better. Men should specialize in baggy corduroy trousers, out-at-the-elbow cardigans and plaid flannel shirts with missing buttons. For women, the uniform is built upon wraparound canvas skirts with pockets spacious enough for balls of twine and clippers or, in winter, much sat-out tweed skirts. Top things off with mismatched, mothy shetlands and gloves that look as though they'd been buried by a puppy after being well chewed.

Casual cocktail conversation should be peppered with mention of ground covers and mulching. Talk about hybridizing (the botanical equivalent of breeding a horse to an ass and getting a mule), hydroponics, succulents, aphids, and bagworms at the dinner table, and you'll be on fertile ground.

Never hesitate to load up at farm stands with strawberries, asparagus, Boston lettuce, and kumquats. Take them home, dump out of original containers and paper and rewrap them in your local newspaper, taking care to make untidy, soggy packages. Hand these out liberally to friends whom you wish to impress. The more out of season the offering, the better ... tomatoes in December, radishes in February. You grew them all under lights in your bathroom.

Finally, try and remember whenever it's a particularly lovely day—sunny, mild, clear as a bell—to respond to any appreciative comment about the weather by saying, "Well, yes, of course, if you don't care about the water table." Since no one has ever *seen* a water table you're 100 percent safe in assuming that it has not been given a thought. "The water table," you tell this feckless horticultural ignoramus, "is really *down*. A nice sunny day is okay if you're only interested in playing golf. But what we *really* need is a good solid week of steady rain."

And what if it's already raining?

Same thing. While everyone else is moaning, squishing around in bubbling shoes and soaked-through clothing, you be sure to let it be known that "we really *need* this rain. Have you any idea how *low* the water table is this month?"

The Book Business ═══════

... a contradiction in terms

*W*hat "business" in the world permits retailers to buy as many pieces as they want, try to sell them and then return them for *full* credit when they can't sell any more? You got it, the book biz. So to discuss books as a business, per se, is a really short conversation. You either accept it or you don't. But should you meet Norman Mailer at a party, and he doesn't feel like hitting you at the moment, here are some things to say to him.

Should you be asked if you've read a particular book, say you read it in galleys (or better yet, manuscript) and you liked it better before the editor got to it.

Express disbelief that Mrs. Onassis works for Doubleday, but say that if she *has* to be in publishing, Doubleday is the right place for her. "I wonder if she does it for the money," you might say, then laugh.

Say that The Literary Guild "has its finger on the pulse of America" but that BOMC (Book-of-the-Month Club, but initials only, please) has cornered a more "upmarket audience."

Talk endlessly about paperback reprint splits, who gets what, Stephen King ("and he's only thirty-four!") and his all-the-rights deal. With more salability comes better splits for the writer—the publisher gets less ("and," you will add, "that's only right").

Say that Knopf used to be a literary house.

Call Simon and Schuster a "factory."

Refer to Harper & Row in the past tense—"They were the dean of American publishers."

Bemoan that fewer and fewer people read, but blame part of it on the high price of books.

Now you and Norman can have a fight. You're equals.

The Movie Biz ══════

. . . look who's calling the shots

*F*irst things first—the uniform gold chains over exposed hairy chest are out, and sunglasses are borderline. A tan is helpful but not imperative. Today's mini-mogul or agent-on-the-way-up is basically tasteful. Just mix in the right "casual" touch with a conservative outfit, for example: pinstripe suit with Adidas on the feet. Preppie stuff is fine if you have a beard and/or carefully coiffed long hair. Stow the Hawaiian shirts, they're passé: the tennis shirt and the cashmere sweater have hung tough. Accessories: a digital watch that does just about everything but windows, and a small vial of fresh Peruvian flake. (*Note:* the watch must be set to LA time if you're in NYC, NYC time if you're in LA.)

You're in the movie business but you don't make movies. You make *deals.* It's a lucrative business, but you don't make money—you make *points* and you win *percentages.* It's important when discussing any movie that you bring in a financial aspect and make that the focus of your conversation. For example, *Jaws*, according to you, is not about a shark, but about "a great job of extensive marketing research," a "beautifully presold package" and "one of the five top-grossing flicks of all time".

Liking or not liking a movie is irrelevant. The emphasis is on having seen movies that haven't been released to the public yet (you "screened the new Warren Beatty picture last week" or "saw it at a preview") and giving flash forecasts ("blockbuster," "stiff," "could break even").

In talking about actors and actresses (known as "the talent") the star is eclipsed in your estimation by his or her agent, i.e.,

Burt Reynolds is "Sue Mengers's [of ICM] hottest property." The talent and the directors (also known as "names") are not seen in terms of quality, but *bankability*, i.e., "Sure, he made *Kane*—but Orson Welles hasn't been bankable for years!" Writers, unless eminently bankable, are irrelevant to the industry and beneath contempt (a standard *in* joke: "Did you hear about the Polish starlet who came to Hollywood—and slept with the writer?").

Nonetheless, the script is where most deals start. It's referred to by you as a *project*, and it's either *in development* (a studio's bought it) or in *turnaround* (up for grabs by other studios). If you have a "hot property" (and, of course you do), you're primarily concerned with the *casting*, the *advertising strategy*, the potential grosses versus the *overhead* and the *bottom line*.

Your Old and New Testament are *Variety* and the *Hollywood Reporter*, respectively. Your patron saints are the Old Hollywood moguls like Thalberg, Goldwyn, and Harry Cohn (who "really knew what pictures are about," as opposed to "the accountants who're running the place these days"). Your attitude is hip, upbeat, but terminally fatigued by jet lag, as you are always just in from or on your way to "the Coast."

It's a crazy business, but you love it. After all, the last time you "four-walled an independent and then got distribution from one of the majors, without a single name in the package," you had "a healthy percentage that yielded five figures."* And that's not bad at all, is it?

Translation: You rented a theater yourself to show a film made outside Hollywood, with no famous people involved in it, and a big studio picked it up, making you lots of moolah 'cause you owned a piece of it.

The Rock Scene ▬▬▬▬

... for the record, you too can be a hip mogul

First of all, we're talking business, not records. Any reference to actual music will give you away. Snob appeal (within a cocaine-crazed crowd) is the order of the day. Never was panache more needed. Here are some great showstoppers to show you off, should you bump into one of the arrogant-oh-so-cool.

- Remember that anything that begins in England is hipper.
- When asked what you think of the new Stones' album, you respond, "It's great, but you should have heard the demos." How much more "in" can you get?
- Find yourself in a discussion of recording technique? "Twenty-four tracks is great, but syncing two sixteen tracks together is unbeatable."
- On the real "business" end of the discussion: "No one is being signed these days, but if they really need you, there's no recession."
- Never bother to learn the names of record company executives; they will have been replaced by the time you get to drop them.
- "Please, I just can't listen to commercial music *at all.*"
- Punk was dead practically before it started; don't refer to it.
- Bands wearing pilot uniforms or aluminum foil are out.
- When confronted with the name of a new group you haven't heard of: "Oh, is ____really good? I haven't heard them; I've been out of town for two weeks." The theory here is that bands come and go so quickly that batting an eye is enough to find you behind. But being elsewhere (unspecified) implies that you're busy and that if the band is really good it will come to you eventually.
- Forget about groups with single-word names, i.e., Styx, Kansas, Kiss. Even the Beatles were *The* Beatles.
- Announce that you're tired of cocaine. This will, if nothing else, get you invited back—your host won't have to share.
- Try not to mention Barry Manilow.
- Wear sunglasses indoors.
- Manners don't count. Having had dinner with Keith Richards counts.

Since rock folk can talk about nothing other than "the biz," you will probably get rapidly bored with the conversation. But what a first impression you've made!

Archaeology ═══════════

. . . can you dig it?

*A*s Jeremy Irons conveyed so clearly in *The French Lieutenant's Woman*, to be an archaeologist is to be excused from many of life's more mundane demands. No need to concern yourself with earning a decent living. A fat grant from the University of Pennsylvania or the National Geographic Society will take care of everyting. No need to attend Cousin Roberta's wedding next month. Your presence is required at the dig when they open the newly discovered burial mound. If you're a bit loose about keeping appointments or paying your bills, don't worry. Everyone knows an archaeologist has more important things on his mind.

Your total involvement in ages past pretty much confers upon you total immunity from responsibility for the here and now. Furthermore, just as it can be said that you never met a playful Doberman or a witty IRS man, so it can be said that no one ever met a frivolous archaeologist. To be considered a professional or even an amateur archaeologist is automatically to be considered thoughtful, scholarly, patient, and hard-working. If you have no other hope of being identified with these virtues, perhaps an archaeological veneer laid over your present existence would do a lot to upgrade you in the eyes of the community.

You begin by taking a hammer to an assortment of used flowerpots. The muddier the better. Having reduced them to a dustpanful of bits and pieces, you then shove them in the oven and bake them at 450° for an hour or so. Remove from the oven, allow to cool, and then lay them out in the lid of a cardboard box, numbering each one in a spidery Spencerian hand. Be careful to cross your sevens and to put top tails on your ones.

The box should be prominently displayed on a windowsill or tabletop. In response to the inevitable questions, you explain that these are shards taken from the Mongollon sites in the American Southwest. Carbon-14 testing dates them somewhere in the Mongollon II period, but the absence of incised designs leads you to suspect that they are more probably of the Mongollon I era.

It's a good idea to get yourself a glass-top coffee table to the underside of which you can attach an aluminum baking tin lined with white surgical cotton. This makes a perfect display case for an assortment of bone bits, pebbles, small twisted pieces of metal (such as might be removed from the key of a coffee can or sardine tin), fragments of seashells, and splinters of glass. Since everything is displayed under glass, nothing can be handled. A good thing, too, since each one is priceless, conveying whole chapters of the past history of the human race.

Keep scattered around in ample evidence such reading matter as *Pueblo Ruins of the Galisteo Basin* by Nelson, *New Perspectives in Archaeology* by Binford and *Pyramids and Temples of Giza* by Petrie (first edition if possible).

Since nowadays you never can tell who is into what, it's altogether possible that you may run into somebody who already knows something about archaeology. If you do, keep your head. A few basic facts should enable you to acquit yourself with flying colors.

"Say what you will about modern technology, radioactive dating processes, and all the rest of it, there just isn't anyone working in the field today who, for sheer brilliance, intuitive intelligence, and downright dedication can hold a candle to good old Sir William [Wm.M.F. Petrie, 1853–1942]. Until he developed the sequence dating system there really was no such thing as truly scientific research."

The mere mention of classical Greek Civilization inevitably evokes a rhapsodic and respectful reaction from everyone, but, as it happens, you're really more interested in *pre*classical Greece, otherwise known as the Dark Age of Greek history. Maybe the period left little in the way of artifacts for present scholars to fiddle with, but "after all, aren't we all indebted to the preclassical era for the present Greek alphabet?"

The Leakeys are hoping you'll be able to drop by the Olduvai Gorge some time before the Tanzanian rainy season for a quick look at a scull fragment they are tentatively identifying as *Zinjanthropus boisei*. You'd certainly like to oblige, but it *is* a long way out there. Besides, with things just opening up right now in the Pampa Grande down in the Lambayeque Valley of Peru, you're just not sure that you're going to make it. At least this year.

Photographs of yourself—out of focus, squinting, a pith helmet pulled low on your forehead, and a chunk of rock held out in front of you—can be variously identified as the dig in Mesopotamia, the Upper Aswan Valley, or Numantia on the upper Duero River in Spain.

You have some strong reservations about the accuracy of thermoluminescence as a dating technique if it's quoted to be anything more exact than 1000 years.

Schliemann's contributions are vastly overrated, and Jim Ford's work was never accorded its just due, at least during his lifetime.

If you ever get the time, you're going to do a biography of Walter Brian Emery, probably Britain's most brilliant Egyptologist. The big question is, can you get all your research into a single volume or will it have to be brought out in two?

Finally, insofar as eastern American coastal prehistory is concerned, it's not the cutback in university funds that bothers you, nor even the careless work habits of today's doctoral candidates when working in situ. Rather, it's the abysmal ignorance of and total indifference to the significance of New York's earliest fossil beds as displayed every day, all over the city, by Con Ed.

7

Competition

Getting in Shape

. . . *pumped pecs and the aerobic way*

*E*ven if your most strenuous activity is getting in and out of taxi cabs, you can Fake It in the world of health and fitness. Just follow the three-step Guaranteed No-Sweat Fitness Program. Remember to take each step slowly. Rome wasn't built in a day. Neither was Arnold Schwarzenegger.

Attitude

Step #1 —

This first, all-important step is designed to give you confidence. God knows you'll need it, looking and feeling as badly as you do. Go out and buy the theme from *Rocky* and *Deutschland, Deutschland Uber Alles*. Play them incessantly for inspiration. Realize that true fitness freaks don't have time to socialize — they're too busy running, race walking, pressing weights, swimming laps, and undergoing physical therapy to go anywhere else. Or else they're just too tuckered out to play. The chances, therefore, are pretty slim of your encountering a bona fide "sweathog" who isn't totally preoccupied with his activity or too out of breath to carry on a decent conversation. Have no fear — you will be able to hold your own in normal circles, where conversation is preferred over perspiration.

Step #2 — No Pain, No Gain

Next, you've got to look the part. Squelch your immediate impulse to splurge on the latest designer warm-up suit, tennis togs, or nifty little shorts with built-in underpants. Only the nouveau jock has a closetful of color-coordinated tops, bottoms, and footwear. The true jock, which is, of course, what you aspire to simulate, began working out long before the gym-dandy look became fashionable. Besides, he or she is basically a slob when in action. What you want is a set of real cotton "sweats." Anything else will brand you a hopeless dilettante or inconsequential novice. Pastel-colored 50/50 poly/cotton sweatshirts that say Jordache on them will only net you directions to the nearest jeans commercial. Your serious sweats should be pure gray (easily accomplished), ill-fitting (ditto — they all are, naturally), torn, worn, and sweat-stained to symbolize the "pain" you've been through. This last criterion is not so easy to meet, as there's nothing like vrai sweat. If you, therefore, must wear a new sweatsuit, at least remember to remove the price tag and wash it in hot water at least 100 times. Then bemoan the fact that your *old* smellies just simply finally "fell apart, the poor things, after all I put them through."

Depending upon your chosen specialty or locale, you can — and should — supplement your basic grays with the acceptable accessories. Runners, for instance, can enliven the overall ensemble with sneakers in colors that nice people never knew existed, let alone dreamed they'd some day be putting on their feet. Tennis players (or any racquet-sport enthusiast) can add a tasteful wristband. Sweatbands will let others know you mean business, no matter what your sport, and leg warmers — these must be squashed uselessly around your calves and ankles — lend a dancerly panache to an otherwise dull picture.

You must, of course, wear your sweatsuit everywhere — to the supermarket, the hairdresser, the movies, and cocktail parties — in order to cultivate the impression that your life and your day revolve around your workouts and you "just don't have time to change." "Life is so much simpler this way, isn't it?" Your misshapen grays will cover up a multitude of sins. Since everyone looks like a sack of potatoes when thus attired, no one will know that underneath lurks not the well-defined body of chiseled muscle marbled with pumped-up veins — but the first-prize winner in the Jell-O look-alike contest.

Failing the acquisition of the aforementioned disgusting garments (or to augment their effect), a "sports-related injury" is a must. Making your entrance on crutches can always be done with panache, especially if you can introduce your companion as your masseur or masseuse. But a strategically placed ace bandage (say, on the knee) and a stoic "Don't worry — the microsurgery was a huge success" will always do in a pinch. Make sure you are prepared with a story of torn ligaments, pulled tendons, bits of dislodged cartilage, because your plight will become the hot topic of the evening. Don't forget to bring your own ice bag "in case it acts up."

Step #3 — The Lingo

Fortunately for you, the world of fitness is filled with words and phrases that can easily be incorporated into any conversation, during any situation. With a little imagination they will not only impress your friends and relatives, but also get you out of many an embarrassing moment.

Carbohydrate loading. Before a competition, athletes stuff themselves with foods rich in starches and sugars to increase their energy. This provides you with a handy way out should you be caught red-handed in the spaghetti pot: "You don't think I want this third helping of fettucini, do you? I *have* to eat this — I'm carb-packing, you know."

Hitting the wall. Though this may sound exactly like the very thing you'd like to do with the next iron-pumper you meet, it is actually the excruciating moment at which a marathoner's muscles finally run out of energy (usually before the twenty-mile mark). Use this catch phrase during any relatively long-distance event such as standing up, or sex: "Gee, my legs feel as though I've hit the wall." Or, "I guess I still haven't recovered from the last time I hit the wall."

Peaking. During the last few days of a training period, athletes perform less work but at a higher intensity. This is supposed to achieve that elusive, delicate point in their development during which they are performing at their mental and physical best, called "the peak." Should your companion's words or actions threaten to upset your (nonexistent) peak, scream at the top of your lungs, "Not now — I'm peaking."

Electrolyte replacement. Every runner worth his salt pills knows that exercise creates an electrolyte imbalance in the muscles. Thus, beer, which is rich in electrolytes, can and should be swilled with heady abandon. Between chugs, you say, "Of course I don't normally quaff three pitchers at one sitting — but I must replace my electrolytes, or I'll really be in trouble."

Fast twitch, slow twitch. Sprinters have an abundance of fast-twitch fibers in their muscles for speed; marathoners have more slow-twitch fibers for endurance. The next time you miss a bus, you have an excuse ready: "We long-distance runners can't have too many fast-twitch fibers, you know." If under certain circumstances you've performed too quickly, it's "because we sprinters never will win prizes in the slow-twitch department."

Runner's high. Enough has been written about this state of euphoria. You can use this term to explain away certain unnaturally cultivated mental states characterized by stupid grins.

Bonking. Not to be confused with runner's high, this condition occurs when the liver runs out of fuel and is characterized by shakiness, dizziness, confusion, lack of coordination. It is often easy to confuse bonking with the advanced states of physical and mental deterioration seen at cocktail parties in full swing. *(Note: It is possible to "bonk" and "hit the wall" at the same time.)*

LSD. The terminally cute abbreviation for *long, slow dis-tance*, as opposed to sprinting. A variation of this is called "Fartlek training," where LSD is alternated with short bursts of gas — er, speed. This technique can be applied to any ac-tivity such as running, swimming, cycling, drinking, eating, sex, paying your taxes, and picking your nose.

Psychocybernetics. This refers to the mental rehearsal, akin to self-hypnosis, that jocks perform to prepare themselves before competition or during a workout. If you're ever caught staring off into never-never land, look stunned and mildly annoyed as you mutter impatiently "psychocybernetics ... mmm."

Should all this faking of fitness leave you as limp as Frank Shorter's T-shirt, don't give up. Even when you're lying face down in a crumpled heap, you can always proclaim, "Me? Don't be silly. Of course I'm alright. I'm an Inner Athlete."

Tennis ═══════════

... it's your serve, ace racqueteer

So full of "experts" is the tennis world — all self-declared, with some of the instant variety and others of long term —

that you can really only count on very brief periods of successful deception. You will, of course, have to pick your moments with great care. Tennis has ballooned to such proportions all over the world that there is almost no place left on earth where you can be absolutely safe from being challenged to show your true worth on some nearby court. However, you should be fairly safe in any of the following situations:

- 22,000 feet up on a transatlantic flight
- on a coffee break talking to a fellow juror of an impounded jury, empaneled for a complex drug smuggling/ murder trial
- visiting a sick friend in the hospital
- talking to somebody's grandmother, but *only* if she's in a wheelchair or on a walker.

Of course you play. But to tell the truth, it's been so long since you played just for the fun of it that you've almost forgotten what it feels like.

If you're under thirty and female, you've been pretty tied up lately working out with Pam (Chrissy, Billie Jean, or Tracy). It takes a lot out of you, but you wouldn't give it up for the world. There's nothing like it to keep your game razor sharp.

If you're over thirty and female, you still work out with Billie Jean but also with Rosie, Margaret, and Kerry.

Kerry?

Kerry Reid. You remember . . . 1977? Eastbourne England? Kerry and Di Fromholtz playing for Australia lost the Federation Cup to the US?

If, on the other hand, you're male and under thirty, your free time has been all tied up in hitting sessions with the Icy Swede, with Roscoe, or Rod.

Over thirty?

Well, whenever you can get away, which nowadays is not too often, you and Bobby like to bum around together. Nothing serious . . . you know Bobby. But now and then you manage to pick up a couple of old duffers like yourselves and have a bit of fun. Why just last week you and Bobby tackled ol' Chuck McKinley and Bob Falkenburg and took them to the cleaners, even though, you must admit, the match went to five sets before you walked off with a 10-8 win in the final set. "That Bobby (head shaking in admiration), he's really something, isn't he?"

If you're winging it within 100 miles of even a half-decent court, you'd be well advised to have one foot swathed in a heavy overlay of bandages and to do all your walking not only with great effort but also with the help of a sturdy cane or crutch. It's a nasty sprain you bad-lucked into last week when you were playing on member-guest day at Palm Springs.

Be philosophical about accepting the sympathy that will come your way. It's probably just as well, as you ease a foot stool or a handy chair under the injured limb. You could really do with a good rest anyhow.

Tennis pros, unlike professional gardeners, stamp collectors, or doctors of philosophy, are all well turned out. And why not? Aren't they all on the take from manufacturers of sport clothes? In fact, although you'd just as soon this wasn't noised around, you've had your entire wardrobe supplied for you for the past four or five years by Head (Slazenger, White Stag, or Bancroft).

"Isn't that the silliest thing you ever heard? But if they think that my wearing their clothers around is good publicity well why should I insist otherwise?" Naturally this means that you are determinedly fashionable: well-cut slacks, good cashmeres, nice tweeds, shoes from either London or Florence (Rome in a pinch) and, knotted casually around the neck, a bit of silk from Liberty or Hermès.

If you're going to risk being seen with a racquet in your hand — something only to be considered in an airline terminal, on a boat pier, or waiting to board the *Orient Express*, make sure that it's not one racquet you're holding but three. It makes no difference if the strings are broken or missing; the heads will be covered with zipper cases anyway. It's a nice touch if you have these inscribed: Forest Hills, Grand Prix Masters, IPAT (Independent Players Association Tournament) or, of course All England Club (purple letters on dark green).

To establish your undeniable intimacy with the game and the greats thereof you should be alert to any possibility of working into your conversations the following:

- Your great-grandfather was taught tennis by none other than Britain's Arthur W. Gore, who, when he was forty-one years old, won the men's singles at Wimbledon (1909). "I guess you might say the game is in the blood."
- Even though you ghosted the writing of Rod Laver's *Education of a Tennis Player*, that doesn't mean you don't think he's one fantastic guy. "I mean off the court as well as on."

If despite your injury and your busy schedule some insensitive, pushy type insists on trying to sign you up for a match on a specific date, don't lose your cool. Just say . . .

- "I'd love to, but I'm leaving for a pro-am tour through eight countries in Europe."
- "I'd love to, but I've promised McEnroe's dad I'd spend the [stated date] with the family to see if I can help the kid work through a troublesome tendency to undercut his backhand net shots."
- "I'd love to, but All American Tennis has hired me as a consultant to take a look at all its operations and make whatever recommendations I think appropriate."

Finally, if you have the bad luck to run into someone else who is obviously one of the greats in the world of tennis, don't let it upset you. Chances are your claim is every bit as good as his/hers.

Baseball

. . . talking a good game

*W*hen Johnny Atanasoff, tinkering around in his mother's garage, came up with the forerunner of today's computer, way back before World War I, little did he realize what he was doing. He thought he was easing the lot of CPAs, electronic engineers, and astronomers. And so he was. But at the same time he was laying the groundwork for something that would reshape the whole mind-set of every baseball buff of the '80s.

Today, baseball and computers belong to each other as totally as the Colonel belongs to the chickens or Henry to the Edsels.

The number of ways that a single nine-inning baseball game can be dismantled, sliced up, and fed into a computer comes closer to infinity than anything encountered in the observatories of Palo Alto or Mount Hale. It's perfectly possible for a couple of baseball freaks, meeting up in a bar, to carry on a conversation composed at least 85 percent of abbreviations and statistical designations. To anyone outside the mystique, it's totally incomprehensible.

Data banks, encyclopedias, and the minds of little kids have been stuffed with just such stuff. It's never in short supply. In fact, by the year 2000, it will surpass the combined volume of statistical data emanating from the UN, Pentagon, and Dow Jones.

If you pause to consider the full import of this fact, you will realize the utter folly of attempting to compete in such an arena. It would be bad enough if you were actually interested in baseball, even enthralled by it. But since it has to be assumed that you couldn't possibly be amused by a game that takes two and a half hours to play and offers nineteen minutes of action, the thought of being sucked into a whirlpool of RBIs, POs, DHs, and ABs is enough to make the mind swirl.

But suppose your boss is a baseball nut? Or the girl you just started dating in a pretty heavy way still has lingering thoughts about the guy she's just left who had two box seats to every Yankee game?

In these or any of a million other cases, it just could behoove you not to be revealed as the total baseball ignoramus that in fact you are. How could you not know or care about that Great American Institution? Indeed, suspicions of subversion and un-Americanism have been seeded by considerably less powerful ammo.

As we've already made clear, under no circumstances should you attempt your Fake It approach in the face of the impenetrable thicket of statistics, records, averages, etc. Any eight-year-old collector of Whacky Paks would see through your sham in less time than it takes to blow one giant-size bubble, pop it, and peel it off his freckled face. Instead, what we're advocating is the oblique approach. We'll begin with something called the *Sporting News*, a newspaper published in St. Louis. It's a weekly, available at any good-size newstand. Buy a copy, roll it up and stuff it in a pocket. Make sure to have the title and logo visible. If you circulate in the company of BB freaks, sooner or later you're going to be asked about it.

"Whatcha got there, ol' buddy? I didn't know you were into baseball. How 'bout that. Do you just pick it up now and then or you a regular reader?"

Try to keep your reply as low-voiced as possible. "Not really. Once in a while they get me to do a piece for them. If I'm not too busy, I try to oblige."

"Wow. No bull? Like what, f'rinstance?"

"Oh-h-h, I don't know. Like What's New In Knucklers, a close-up of those fabulous Niekro brothers, Phil and Tom. Or an interview with Catto Pesacto, Puerto Rico's sweetheart."

Don't bother to bone up on what the facts are behind those pieces of baseball journalism. There really is no need. Your statements alone convey such an insider's knowledge that no right minded baseball buff would ever press you for verification.

If you find yourself in the personal digs of any real baseball nut, look around for a huge, fat book that's sure to be not far off: *The Baseball Encyclopedia*. Flip back the cover for a quick look at the edition and then, depending on what you find, choose one of the following:

- "Hm-m-m. Too bad you have the second [third] edition here."
- "Hm-m-m. Nice, this fifth edition. Better than the fourth, of course, and you can take the second and third . . . no damned good at all."
- "Hm-m-m. First edition? If you're really serious about the game, you actually should junk this and get the fifth. If you're serious, that is."

Of course, most baseball talk has to do with verbal replays of last night's game, speculation about tomorrow's game and, as might be expected, absolutely *endless* speculation as to how the teams will end up when the season draws to a close. You can afford to stay aloof from all this, to tune out completely, provided you have a couple of fallback comments to make when your turn comes around. Commit a few of the following to memory, and you're sure to emerge with rep intact:

- "Why talk fix, bribe, or bought? What could ever be mentioned in the same breath with the Black Sox Scandal, when that bastard Shoeless Joe threw the Series game?"
- "Don't give me that sold-down-the-river stuff. You must have completely blotted out the Great Betrayal perpetrated by that rat Walter O'Malley when he hauled the Dodgers out of Brooklyn and sold them into slavery out in LA."

- "Don't talk dirty ball to me. I was there the night Graig Nettles popped a fly and his bat broke into a zillion pieces. Damned if he hadn't reamed it out and stuffed it full of cork to get more zing. Even over in the dugout we were snowed out in a blizzard of cork guts."
- "Never mind Valenzuela. What about Ryne Duren? He was legally blind and continued to pitch for the Yankees." (This is a particularly good point for women to make.)

If you have the bad luck to fall in with won't-shut-up baseball nuts and you see no hope of extricating yourself from their company — or their company from the subject — you can always announce that insofar as you're concerned, the *real* interest in the game resides not in the Major Leagues (the American is not worth your time, anyway; it's been nowhere since Ruth and Gehrig threw in their bats) but rather in "Triple A ball. That's where the future's at, you know."

Since 99 percent of all BB freaks are exhaustively following the race for the pennant, chances are they won't know beans about the farm teams, of which, of course, the Triple A's are the best. You should therefore be able to wing your way without too much difficulty.

No matter how you try, you're just about certain, somewhere along the way, to get immersed in the verbal battle of records. It's a bore but unavoidable.

Instead of boning up on the obvious ones, Hank Aaron as the game's leading hitter or Dave Winfield as the game's highest paid player, you should go for the more obscure records, hallowed by the passage of time. Any of the following will do the trick:

- The only three-brother outfield to play in the Major Leagues: Jesus, Matt, and Felipe Alou.
- History's first pinch hitter: "Smiling" Mickey Welch for the New York Giants in 1889.

- Most grand slams in one career: Lou Gehrig — twenty-three.

Since baseball is actually just an enormous elaboration of pitch and hit, it's important to be able to show a casual but total grasp of pitches: split-fingered fastballs, scuff balls, dirty-double-fingered forkballs, screwballs, beanballs, brushbacks, change ups, and sinkers. You refer to various hits as screamers, dribblers, trolley lines, and scratch singles. When you speak of a home run, you lower your voice to achieve maximum dramatic tension and then you allude to the hitter who "sends it downtown."

Finally, even if you've tried the whole of your adult life to ignore the myths and headlines of baseball, you still must know that this Great American Pastime marches to the papal drumming of someone called a "commissioner." Since there have only been five such totems in the history of the game, it's no trick at all to pass yourself off as conversant with every one of them. First, Judge Landis, called the Savior of Baseball by anyone who *thinks* he knows his baseball, but otherwise known as a Meatax judge by the true insider. Then came Happy Chandler, Ford Frick, and a retired Air Force general called Eckert. Right now there's Bowie Kuhn, whom you hate because he's thrown in his hand with the Lords of Baseball, otherwise known as the owners. . . .

8
Toys

Wheels ▬▬▬▬▬▬▬

. . . you are what you drive

When someone asks you what kind of car you have, do you say "blue"? Do other motorists speed away when they see you driving toward them, fearful that anyone driving a piece of tin like yours will have no respect for them? When you bring your car for a tune-up, does the garage mechanic tell you not to bother? If your answer to any of these questions is "yes," you need this chapter badly. Of course you don't have to actually *own* a fabulous car — this is not a book devoted to consumerism. It is, if you remember correctly, devoted to helping you make a grand impression with panache. So here goes.

You are at a ritzy party and have already bowled over the people around you with your knowledge of wine, horiticulture, and many other things. Suddenly you are asked (do not offer the information) what kind of car you drive.

"Up until a few months ago I drove a Lamborghini, but there are no really good mechanics in the United States, and it eventually proved to be impractical."

To be sure, the folks near you now understand what league you're playing in. Move in for the kill.

"I am, however, really happy with my Ferrari Boxer. I didn't know luxury until I discovered the flat 12."

It doesn't matter what that means (it actually refers to the number of cylinders, which allow the car to go 200 mph); it implies wealth, exclusivity (there are fewer than 100 of these cars in the United States) and a knowledge of the practical. The Ferrari Boxer, by the way, costs well over 100 grand. Your hope is that the people around you will know that; it's not the kind of thing you'd ever bring up. You might want to mention, though, that it doesn't "corner" as well as your Porsche Turbo.

It also isn't bad to have a little practical, or everyday, knowledge. Were you to mention that the Slant Six is a wonderful, reliable engine (made by the Chrysler Corporation), it wouldn't hurt. Similarly, if you were to say that Cadillacs and Lincoln Continentals are worth the money you pay for them, you'd be right.

Diesel engines? They're very up-and-coming, and no real tune-up is ever necessary. They're "easy to run."

If you really must avoid the whole discussion, you can go back to the opening question, above, and actually say "blue." Or you can say that your driver (not chauffeur — outdated) takes care of everything, and that the whole subject is beneath you. If the Lord had wanted you to drive, he would have made *you* a car.

Computers ═══════════

... getting your data together

A computer illiterate.

There it is ... as damning an accusation as you're going to come across. At least for now and probably right up until such time as you can be called an interplanetary ignoramus.

Nor should it cheer you up to know that there are fewer

and fewer functional computer illiterates around. Even little kids are spinning video discs to come up with all sorts of intricate answers to all sorts of questions that most of us wouldn't even know how to ask, much less answer.

If you've been sailing along under the idiotic illusion that simply by knowing the name of Columbus's first mate on the second of his three voyages or by being able to finger your way through Beethoven's *Minuet in G* you could pass yourself off as *educated*, well, you're in, to coin a phrase, for a rude awakening. Today, it's not a nodding acquaintance with Pliny the Elder nor a knack for discussing for forty-five insouciant seconds the psychological implications of Piscasso's blue years that's going to win you any sort of kudos in the circles that really count.

Rather, it's being on a first-name basis with Booz, Allen & Hamilton (consultants). It's being able to chat amusingly about having been psychoanalyzed by Weizenbaum's *ELIZA*. It's being able to look someone right in the eye and tell them that you've fallen out of love with IBM System 3 and you're now really into some very heavy feelings with Control Data Cyber 171.

It's a given that nowadays, with places like MIT, Carnegie-Mellon, and Stanford spewing out an evergrowing stream of real-live people who have substituted diodes for adenoids, people for whom a byte is not a piece of your doughnut but a grouping of eight bits, it's going to be more and more difficult for people like yourself to hold your own in any group that could be classified, even loosely speaking, as upwardly mobile.

Furthermore, faking it in this kind of heady company is *not* easy. The first thing you should accept as axiomatic is that even a smidge too much is going to sink you. Let's say, for instance, that you're in Stage #1 of what could turn out to be a truly meaningful relationship. Dinner was a big success, you both laughed at the same Woody Allen one-liners, and later you uncovered the absolutely amazing coincidences that you both think Jacques Tati is a comic genius and neither one of you can stand Norman Mailer, Christo, or any of Fellini's last five films.

Obviously things are going along really well.

"You might almost say," you venture, "that what we have here is compatible hardware architecture." As computerish a phrase as one could hope for at 11:45 on a Saturday night.

But see what happens. . . .

The pillows tumble to the floor. A heedless elbow upsets the chilled bottle of Zinfandel, the light dimmer is spun back up and your date pipes up, "What do you think the chances are of Schank smoothing the kinks out of FRUMP?"

Clearly, your mistake was to steer your conversational ship into waters where you were ill-prepared to drop anchor.

In any case, one-on-one computer faking it is at best tricky. If you keep it out in the open, well hedged by a dog-eat-dog group in which every single person is hell-bent on displaying his or her own expertise you sharply reduce the chance of being caught with your buffers down.

Never the head-on approach. Rather, "I remember lunching one day just off campus with Eddie Feigenbaum. He was just nuts about tortillas ... not the crispy kind but, you know, those very chewy ..."

There you are. You've established your intimacy with one of the country's numero-uno biggies in the world of computers, and now all you have to do is help out the helpless by identifying the campus as Stanford and then swing right into a list of the three or four different Tex-Mex wholesale grocers where you can order those chewy tortillas by the case.

Or you can try, "I bet Charlie Lecht ten bucks that ACT would go to seventy times earning as soon as he went public. When he paid me the ten spot we were on the Eastern shuttle circling Logan in a pea-souper, and since I just happened to have one of these little Texas Instruments pocket calculators on me, we started gin rummying on it, and the next thing I knew we were coming in for a landing in Syracuse and I'd parlayed the ten into almost $200. But anyone who's ever been in Syracuse knows perfectly well ..."

The trick, you see, is to flaunt your computer expertise with little sideways allusions.

- "Minsky was always trying to convince me that ..."
- "Arthur D. Little sends out these incredible headhunters."

Believe us, until you've had one of these guys on your tail you just don't know what high octane is. And no matter how often you send them packing, wait a month, maybe two, an whad-daya know? There they are, right back on your doorstep ... contract in hand and the perks that go with it. It's fine if a Ferrari, a chalet in St. Anton, and a season box for at-home Red Sox games is all you want out of life. And, obviously, there must be some types that fall for that kind of thing. Otherwise, Arthur D. Little being Arthur D. Little, why of course they'd come up with a different approach. I mean, can't they always just program all their needs into their LARC and come up with whatever kind of recruitment program they need or want, huh?"

If you play your hand so inexpertly as to find yourself face to face with a genuine computer wiz — not nearly so unlikely a possibility as you would like to think — your best out is to kid around about Boolean algebra and bubble memory, establishing from the outset your determination *never* to be serious about something as important in your life as your computer interrelationships. After all, you don't pray in public, do you?

So it's hi-ho-hum about your COBOL, and it's eyes rolled skyward if you even have to think about your LISP or your LOGO.

Should an inquisitor persist, you've only to say that "one more word, and I mean even one, and I'll go straight into GLITCH," which, if he knows anything at all, will tell him that complete shutdown of all systems is imminent.

On the other hand, should you find yourself so fortunate as to be closeted with a total neophyte, computerwise (as they say), and you're absolutely certain it's not a case of dissembling, by all means feel free to loosen up:

- "The heuristic approach to problem-solving, if you're the least bit creative ... well, let's just say it's not the most gratifying."
- "If any of this high-tech stuff begins to get ahead of you, my advice is just to fall back into the lap of the mnemonics. I mean, you can't get in much trouble there, now can you?"
- "Could you wait just the tiniest little nanosec until I wiggle out of this ..."

- "What's pico sec one way or the other if two people really feel ready to go from A to D?"
- "Let's not slide over into encryption if our input-output transducers aren't in sync."

Faking it in the nether world of time sharing and software, of McGurk and McColough, of Datapro, Datran, and EFT systems, calls for a steady hand, a sure eye and, when things go awry, a fleet foot.

But it's an area in which a faker can always draw consolation from the ever-present possibility of feeding all the variables into a mess of microcircuitry and getting in return one's very own custom-made program.

Horses

. . . racing, fox hunting, polo . . . the sporting way of all equine flesh

*F*lair, style, and panache in the horse world is infinitely preferable to underplaying it straight. The true haute monde of horses is nippy, kicky, and bucky. Keep your distance. No need to approach. Armed with just a few tips, there's not a reason in the world why you shouldn't hold your own in the mink 'n' manure set, should the mood strike.

First off, understand that there are only three milieus you even recognize:

- thoroughbred horse racing
- fox hunting
- polo

And forget about ever stopping to stroke the nose of a cop's horse. No person of substance would ever do that. Walk straight past, eyes front. For you, a cop's horse doesn't count *at all.*

Thoroughbred Horse Racing

From a pawn shop or a lost and found in a railroad station, get yourself a pair of good binoculars with carrying strap. No matter if the innards have fallen out; you carry them for effect only. Round out the "look" with a tweed cap, tattersall waistcoat, nicely formless Harris Tweed jacket and, for your buttonhole, a small gold-and-enamel button that (from a distance, anyway) verifies you as a lifelong member of all the best turf-and-field clubs. If you're female, go Poochy-Goochy.

At the track, ignore the claiming races. The elite, of which you now are a member, go to the track to watch only one or two of the eight or nine races. While the platers and four-year-old maidens are slogging around the oval, you are sitting at your luncheon table, on the rail, and as close to the finish line as you can manage. You are studying the form. Only the peasants bet every race.

Before the Big Race, amble down to the paddock. Only owners and trainers are admitted inside the enclosure, but, if you handle the situation properly, you should be able to make it past the attendant simply by flicking your lapel button. Engaging an owner in serious dialogue as the two of you approach the paddock entrance should also get you through.

Once inside the enclosure, you're in fine shape to hobnob

with your peers. In this area only two things count: breeding and conformation. No need to know anything about either. There's more inbreeding among thoroughbreds than there was among the pharaohs of Egypt. One or two sires really account for all the horses racing today, so if you mention either one, you're sure to be safe.

"You can always tell that Omaha line."

"The Hyperion blood comes through every time."

Before the jockeys mount, the horses will circle the enclosure, led by handlers. This gives you a chance to stand off, eyes narrowed, head tilted ever so slightly. You're studying the conformation.

"Good shoulder on that filly there."

"I like the way he carries his head."

"Nice action there."

Always best to say too little rather than too much. You've only to call a filly a gelding or refer to a shank as a leash and your hash is cooked.

Real horse people are verbal tightwads at the track. Do the best you can to sneak a look at a good trainer's program and mark your own program accordingly, but keep your markings to yourself. If asked point blank to show your choices, just smile and stuff the program in your pocket. "I wouldn't want to change the odds" will get you out of that one.

Avoid the lines in front of the $2 windows.

Being seen in the lines for the $50 or $100 windows, acting casual, can't hurt. Of course, if you can manage to be seen turning away from one of those big-time windows, rifling through a wad of big ones, that's just dandy. Thoroughbred racing is the most snobbish of all sports, pretending all the while to be the most democratic. In other words, there's no harm at all in your dropping a friendly word to the boozy-looking bum who's peddling tout sheets by the entrance to the club house. A cheerful greeting to anyone who's bowlegged and under five feet suggests you know the fraternity of retired jockeys, a sure sign of an "in."

Speak to all track attendants, waiters, and ushers — not in depth, of course, but just a word or two in passing to confirm that you are an experienced race goer.

For those moments when you want very much to be over-heard, spike your conversation with one of the following stock phrases, and you'll at once be recognized for what you are:

- "Actually, I'm considering not even shipping at all to Saratoga this year."
- "We're breeding for distance this time around."
- "If you don't have a good boy aboard, the best trainer in the world won't win the race for you."
- "Of course, if you're willing to drop in class . . ."

Here are some rules *never* to be broken:

- Don't cheer. No "Atta boy" or "Give 'im the whip." Orderly applause as something trots back to the winner's circle is all right and suggests your choice was the right one.

- *Never* call them "ponies." Ever.
- Speak of the "boy," not the "jockey."

And for conversation purposes, remember:

- *Belmont:* Too big business for my tastes.
- *Saratoga:* I never miss the week of the yearling sales, do you?
- *Delaware:* Love it! Reminds me of going to the track with my father as a child. (Since persons under twenty-one are not allowed at tracks, it's implicit that your father was very definitely a racing VIP.)
- *Pimlico:* Still a touch of charm there.
- *Hialeah:* Remember how it used to be? Before . . .
- *Lincoln Downs:* Where's that?
- *Santa Anita:* Ah, those mountains in the background.
- *Aqueduct:* Pardon me?

Fox Hunting

For this, go out and buy the most expensive Liberty silk oversize square you can find. Fold it into a triangle. Stick your left arm into it and knot it behind your neck. You're now ready to speak with authority and, if you follow these instructions, ready to be listened to.

First of all, your injury. No, you *do not* allude to it. No details, please. No corny, you-should-see-the-other-guy jokes. Anyway the "other guy" is of course a horse. A British-style stiff upper lip for this one.

"I'll be out exercising before the week's out." (Exercising *horses*, not yourself, but certainly don't explain — your listener will understand at once.)

A cheery "slight difference of opinion" will also do nicely.

Gauge yourself carefully. Draw out your opponent. Find out which hunt he "rides with" and after he's waxed eloquent, just say, "Is it live or drag?"

Whichever it is, suggest you prefer the other, using either of the two following reasons:

- "I'm afraid I still prefer the real thing. Outguessing the fox is almost as much fun as the chase itself. Silly of me, I know."
- "Of course live is the most *authentic*, but I'm afraid I still prefer the faster pace of the drag. Silly of me, I know."

From church fairs and flea markets pick up faded, brown photographs of small children in curls astride shaggy ponies, preferably being led by a groom. Have them nicely framed and hung on poorly lit walls of your house. No need to caption. The meaning is clear.

Fill the top shelf of your coat closet with "hard hats," which in this case means rigid-crown derbies and steel-reinforced velvet-covered caps. Arrange them so that anyone opening the closet to hang up a coat will be showered with falling hats.

Avoid too neat a dwelling. Fox hunters are never picky, prefering the rough 'n' ready look. Pint-size bottles of liniment rub and ten-inch-wide ace-bandage rolls on your mantelpiece are just right. Boots are called for, of course, but God forbid that in the requisite heaps beside both the front and back doors you should have a single high-heeled cowboy boot. *Never!* On the matter of spurs, if you can find the proper variety, i.e., blunt, slightly turned-down ones, fine. But the risk is too great that you'll turn up with Pancho Villas stabbers, which would queer you forever in the fox-hunting world — a world, we hasten to add, in which a successful fake reaps splendid dividends.

Despite their casual households, fox hunters dine well and drink well. Also copiously. All those old English hunting prints with servants passing stirrup cups to mutton-chopped gents astride bow-necked horses, well it's a tradition that's never vanished. Few social events are more satisfying than stomping around on highly polished parquet floors in your muddy boots, accepting offerings of Smithfield ham or Stilton on toast while waiting to be called in for the afterhunt buffet.

Sleeping around is every bit as much of the fun as eating around. Any member of any hunt will welcome your staying the night if you just explain that "my man is vanning my horse in the morning." It would be inhospitable to refuse bed and board to *anyone* making such a request.

"But what if I should actually have to get on a horse?" you might ask.

Definitely a situation to be avoided. At the first toot of the master's horn or the first yip of a hound, even the most woebegone old nag will in all probability come alarmingly to life, pawing the ground, breaking into a sweat and jangling the bit between its enormous yellow teeth, as if in preparation for instant flight — an accurate assessment.

You may well have to tough this situation out, so hunch down in the saddle, take a good firm short hold on the reins along with a generous fistful of mane.

Hands down, shoulders back, knees in, and start praying.

You may well find that all efforts to pull away from the crowd to head for the privacy of a nearby barn, the protection offered by a thick stand of pines, or even an uncut cornfield are to no avail. Horses like to stay with each other, even if it means tailing one another over stone walls and very solidly built split-rail fences.

Bailing out (yes, that's acceptable terminology though unacceptable practice) if the pace gets too much for you should only be considered if you're out of sight. Performing this act before an on-galloping group of your peers can result only in irreversible defrocking.

As to what to wear, go to the most expensive saddlery shop you can find. Tell the manager you're interested in both rat catcher and formal. *He'll* know. "I've lost thirty pounds these last few weeks training for our local hunt meet (that mean's once-a-year race), so I guess I'd best start all over from scratch."

You'll be made to sit astride a headless, tailless horse whilst being measured for britches. You'll have to flex your knees, hunch your shoulders, "stand high in your irons, if you please, sir (madam)." Keep a sharp eye on all the paraphernalia that's brought out for your approval. Avoid any down payments, and as soon as the tape measure is removed, hurry over to the biggest and best hospital thrift shop. There you're almost certain to find every article of clothing for which you've just been fitted. Widows donate, and since fox-hunting husbands not infrequently expire in private rooms of very expensive hospitals, it's not too surprising that the surviving spouse orders the butler to clear out "everything and don't forget the tax exemption form." You may have to shop around a bit in order to find things in your proper size, but persistence pays off; britches, boots, waistcoat, stock, pink coat, and top hat can easily set you back three grand. And that's not counting the horse.

For casual exchanges while waiting for the hunt to assemble, the following should do nicely:

- "Some people don't mind a cold-blooded horse (an equine version of a mutt), but I still prefer the clean bred."
- "Lovely country down there around Aiken."
- "Myopia? Yes, of course. As a matter of fact I grew up there, hunted the same pony until I was ten."
- "Deep Run? The MFH (Master of Fox Hounds) and I roomed together at school." (Be careful here not to say *college.* To a man jack (jill), fox hunters practice ongoing illiteracy.)
- "This horse I'm on? I promised to try him out for a friend. You don't think otherwise I'd ever throw a leg over something that looks like *this?*"
- "My own hunt? A small pack about fifty miles west of Washington, D.C. (London, Dublin, Lexington, Warrenton, Cork, or Philadelphia . . . whichever is farthest)."

If you can sustain the ploy of the broken wing in the expensive silk sling, then by all means let it be known that you're interested in "following in the morning by motorcar." (Such antique expressions are all to the good in your effort to "pass" among the fox hunters.) Your request will in all likelihood secure you the offer of a car *and* a guide, both of which should be accepted "because, as a matter of fact, I've heard your country's very trappy." (Never mind what it means, they'll love it.)

At drink-eat time — the end of the day — jostle into the open house right along with all the others and tell anyone you see that "I liked the way you handled that post and rail this morning," and you'll not only be believed but you'll be loved as well.

Before departing, go up and tell the MFH how much you've enjoyed your stay and that you look forward to "having your hunt with us," adding, "and of course we'll be glad to mount you."

Polo

This is the last and most dangerous horse field for fakers. For starters, it's advisable to get rid of everything that resembles polo clothing: lightweight britches, all T-shirts except perhaps those that proclaim devotion to rock bands and Eastern gurus, all boots and, of course, any of those hard cork hats you see strapped onto the heads of Prince Charles and the like. It's all right to have an umbrella stand full of long mallets and a heap of soiled checked coolers (lightweight horse blankets) dumped in a corner of your hall. But anything more suggestive of active participation is just too risky.

Where do you usually play?

(As far away from here as I can get.) Actually, you have to say, "Oh, in Westbury," or "Oh, in Palm Beach," or "Oh, in Windsor Park," or, "To tell you the truth, I haven't played much since I left Princeton (the Point, or VMI)."

Polo, which is actually expensive croquet on horseback, is scarce. If you're careful as to just where you try to fake your expertise, you'll probably get away with it. Silk foulards, casually knotted at the throat (but safely pinned to your undershirt underneath), and $200 cashmere sweaters looped over your shoulders and knotted by the sleeves around your neck will always help.

In this league, you *can* refer to a grownup horse as a "pony." Some of these "ponies" are huge, so it's more of a euphemism than anything else. The best players are Argentinian, Italian,

English, and South African. Americans hardly count at all. The French try, but the game requires just a mite more interpersonal cooperation than the French are willing to put into it.

What the Babe was to baseball, so Sonny was to polo. Use his name freely. (It's Ruth and Bostwick, respectively.) Also, since he's dead, you enjoy immunity from challenge.

Just as golf provides a handicap of strokes, so does polo provide a handicap of goals, but, unlike golf, there is a top handicap: ten. To be a ten-goal player is to be the best there is. For your needs, probably seven or eight is all you should claim. If you're speaking to someone who knows anything about polo (obviously a situation you should avoid), find out if your counterpart plays the game indoors or outdoors, and then identify yourself with the opposite. For some reason, indoor players don't mess around out of doors, and the outdoor players never do it indoors. If you claim indoor ranking, you'll have been playing in armories, so be prepared to speak of the uptown or the downtown armories; armories out in the boondocks don't count at all.

Here, again, try to secure a faded, out-of-focus photograph of a team grinning into the camera, squinting, and clinging to a silver loving cup, this time with scrawled, illegible signatures. "Even my mother couldn't tell which one was me." There, of course, is your name, plain as anything. A good place to hang the artifact is on the lavatory wall. Sooner or later, everyone goes there, usually alone and with ample time to study the evidence.

The most important thing to remember about polo is that it's always played in good-weather places. You just don't ever see teams slugging it out amidst snow drifts and icicles. So any time you get a really good tan away from home, you capitalize on it by allowing that you're only just back from a polo tour with your team. Buenos Aires, Auckland, Jo'burg — they're all decently distant and just what the situation calls for.

Finally . . .

Faking it is always risky. Faking it in the horse world is risky in the extreme. Horses are dangerous, and although the pay-offs can be fantastic — acquired charisma, freeloading options, and exotic but becoming clothing — the chance of being permanently maimed is very real. Horses may be romantic to consider from a distance, but as Shakespeare himself said, "Both ends are dangerous and the middle's uncomfortable," so you're certainly wise either to avoid the subject altogether or to Fake It . . . but *carefully*.

9
Let's Get Serious

Astrology

. . . the weirdest science

N ever mind about what moon is in whose house. Leave
that to the hard-core and the faintly loony — the people with
charts. What you want to do here is either dismiss the whole
thing (i.e.: When asked what your sign is, answer, "The best")
or make a bit of sense, if humanly possible. Here are the proper
clichés, sign by sign:

Aquarius (January 20 — February 18) Creative and mod-
ern-thinking. Often mistaken for not-too-bright. Does not learn
from experience.

Pisces (February 19 — March 20) Emotionally powerful,
if a bit paranoid. Makes up by being a bully for what lacks in
real bravery. Has no pets.

Aries (March 21 — April 19) Outdoorsy and independent.
Walks away rather than have a decent discussion.

Taurus (April 20 — May 20) Great stick-with-it-ness. Often
wealthy later in life, usually through crooked means.

Gemini (May 21 — June 20) Intelligent, if schizophrenic.
Neither aspect of personality admirable. Fast at making deals,
fast at losing friends.

Cancer (June 21 — July 22) A good listener, easy to take
advantage of. Wildly emotional, barely able to function in adult
environment.

Leo (July 23 — August 22) Stubborn and forceful. Seems
to listen but doesn't really care. Makes good cop.

Virgo (August 23 — September 22) Weighs facts carefully, often resulting in complete inaction. Obsessively clean and hard to be with because of it.

Libra (September 23 — October 22) Sensitive to music, art, and literature. Happy completely alone, making everyone grateful for it.

Scorpio (October 23 — November 21) One-way sensitivity. Easily hurt, but unconscious of others' feelings. Makes excellent file clerk.

Sagittarius (November 22–December 21) Loves to gamble, often loses. Sees the bright side of everything, however senseless.

Capricorn (December 22–January 19) Tends to be private and as a result, learns little. Is best as child.

Enough?

Psychiatry/Psychology

. . . head trips and tricks

*T*he evening is shaping up. Definitely. The vibes are good, the prelims are over. From here on in it all looks A-1 mellow.

The talk is easy, the group is small, lots of laughs, everyone getting through to everyone else. There's no reason not to think that somewhere in the not too distant future there might very well be the beginnings of an altogether satisfactory relationship.

Until . . .

Chances are it's only a stray word, an insignificant gesture, that triggers it, but once underway, there's not the slightest chance of throwing matters into convivial reverse.

"Have you discussed that with your analyst?" you hear.

"Certainly. We've been working through it for the last half dozen sessions."

"Yeah. I achieved resolution last year. You're going to find it a very high energy experience. Very peak."

Of course, the preceding exchange can come across in any one of a zillion variations. The trick is to catch it in its very first, newborn moments, because if you let it slip by unnoticed, let it swell from a limp, amorphous verbal nothing into a huge, globular, attention-getting, deflation-proof balloon, you can kiss good-bye every one of the evening's sweet promises. Because what is happening is going to continue to happen, with or without your assistance. What you have here is a case where if you're not with it, you're hopelessly, irrevocably without it. In less time than it takes to spell *Sigmund,* the conversation is going to turn and sweep like a flash flood over territory that not only is unexplored but is more full of booby traps than a USMC obstacle course.

Like it or not, we live in an age where psychological reality carries more whammy than a pie in the face or a kick in the pants. Furthermore, any suggestion that you have been going, day to day, sorting out what is from what ain't *without* professional guidance of one sort or another . . . well, it's just nothing that you want to have to fess up to. Especially once someone in the crowd trots out for group admiration and approval his or her revelations as harvested on the couch.

"At sixty-five dollars an hour?" With car payments, a suspended Visa card, an impending second mortgage, possibly root canal work, and a scheduled hearing with the IRS, who's going to sign up for that kind of open-ended financial commitment?

It's an understandable argument, but unfortunately it's also so square, so unchic, so totally "out of it" that by far your best bet is to forget it before you even begin it.

Psycho-anything — therapy, somatic, neurotic, analysis —is just another way of writing $$$$$$$$$$$, which of course is part of its charm. To be "in analysis" most conclusively dubs you as a big spender. It's right up there with having a 100-foot yacht chafing at your moorings or a string of polo ponies nickering away in your barn.

It further suggests that you're a person for whom time, that unpleasant tyrannizer of the working class, holds no threat, because whoever brought their id and egos into alignment in a couple of $1.98 quickie sessions?

So, if you've had no personal experience with psychiatry, psychology, analysis — Freudian, Adlerian, Jungian, or otherwise — it's obvious that you are going to have to fake it.

Don't be nervous. Just a few stock phrases will get you launched. Fortunately, unlike rocketry, trout fishing, or accounting, *feelings* take precedent over *facts*, generalities outrank specifics.

You establish your credentials with something simple:

- "Don't you find the language of behaviorism excessively arid?"
- "I'm not sure if I really agree with such neo-Freudians as Adler and Fromm."
- "I guess I have trouble relating to nonpsychoanalytic thinkers like Maslow or Carl Rogers."

Once the ball starts rolling, you'll find your input can be quite minimal provided it's punctuated by one of a dozen or so phrases:

- objectified feelings
- overcoming castration anxiety
- the ineffable revelation
- my rebirthing process
- repression, regression, and the Oedipal compulsion.

If pressed for clarification of anything, you can either freewheel it, or, if sensing yourself on thinning ice, you can quite legitimately take refuge in a murmured suggestion that until you've worked your way through a somewhat difficult impasse, you'd prefer not to explore the subject in any greater depth. In contrast to desirable procedures in, say, tennis or checkers, the act of retreating in the face of a discussion about your own psychoanalytical experience will win you the respectful understanding of your audience. Retreat therefore should be considered a legitimate and immediately available option.

The whole world of psychology and psychiatry is more splintered than a seaside boardwalk. If you should happen to stumble across someone who seems to have secured even a tentative grip on any one particular brand of shrinkdom, you have only to veer smoothly off in another direction, confident that no good Rolfian is going to be able to chase after a primal screamer, no follower of est is going to know beans about drama therapy or the satisfactions of biorhythms.

Except for California and New York, the whole American shrink situation is still pretty much in its Kitty Hawk days. This is a fact of life that strongly suggests the obvious good sense of pursuing this subject only in places like Kenne-bunkport, Biloxi, or Spokane. If, however, you have the misfortune to get yourself into a conversation with someone who seems to have some honest-to-God firsthand knowledge of the subject, you should without hesitation throw your entire grasp of matters into the Viennese arena. Getting shrunk either in Vienna or by a Viennese is something of an ultimate, positively guaranteed to earn you top-dog slot in any discussion.

- "If it hadn't been for Dr. Schnitzel, I probably would never have worked out my transference."
- "Once Dr. Hasenpffer and I managed to move out of repression and into acceptance of ego autonomy, I really started making tracks."

It's not just one's personal experience that rates. It's also being casually conversant with the entire shrink business. If, for instance, you can (in an offhand way) compare Kirkegaard to Wittgenstein, Eric Berne to R.D. Laing or all of them to Karen Horney, well, you're just about certain to carry the conversational ball right over into the end zone, making the extra point with nothing more arduous than a Freudian drop-kick.

Samples:

- "Ad hoc definitions are meaningless to someone like myself who is only just now coming to terms with the persistence of the unconscious."
- "Didn't Freud prove to us once and for all that the origins of our sexual proclivities are not to be found in our conscious choices? Hmm?"

Direct questions about your personal situation are very bad form. Very bad. Confronted with such a question, it's best to either look pained or ignore it. If neither approach nor avoidance seems to do the trick, then it's best to wing it, remembering all the while that you're dealing with a subject where "murky" is the norm and "incomprehensible" is daily fare. For example:

Q. "Does your analyst believe in soliloquy therapy?"

A. "Mine does. But my girlfriend's doesn't. But we're trying to work through to an acceptable level of psychotherapeutic compromise."

Finally, do please remember that in this league the most demeaning thing you can be called — the lowest status to which you can be reduced — is *normal*. Similarly, being called paranoid, schizo, or just plain bananas has to be seen as an all-out, 100 percent compliment.

Nonsailing

. . . let's hear it for the landlubber

This chapter is being included as the result of an in-depth study commissioned by our publisher. In an effort to determine the area in which lay the greatest need for a reference book of this sort, they approached the IBM Systems Research Institute, which in turn proceeded to conduct a three-year work-study program. The results of the research were then cross-checked and correlated with the findings of an MIT research-grant team delegated to cover the same material. From this exhaustive research a clear pattern emerged: It became apparent that the greatest area of abuse and hardship in modern-day society arises from the practice of amateur sailors impressing fellow citizens into their vocation, usually against their will. The average victim is a well-meaning human being who, through inadvertence or ignorance, falls into the hands of amateur sailing maniacs.

Intending only to be courteous, the victim will modestly allow that he did indeed win the Sailing Cup at Camp Wingaway, the under-fourteen class. Or perhaps that he still remembers fondly a sunset sail somewhere off the west coast of Florida with a friend whose name he's long since forgotten.

These are ordinary conversational tidbits of no intended consequence. Yet all too often such entirely innocent disclosures result in the victim's being roped into a sailing holiday, one week to do the Long Island-Connecticut shoreline, and maybe up through the Cape canal if the weather holds. People who offer such invitations, as the studies clearly showed, are impervious to denials, assertion, or proclamations of limited seamanship. They simply won't take No for an answer.

"I have this little sweetheart of a thirty-five foot sloop. She really sails herself. You'll see . . ."

And see you will. For all your protests, your denial of any serious seagoing knowledge, you're all too apt to find yourself alone at the helm in a heavy sea with the winds rising, the glass dropping, and the skipper/host down below deck rooting through his sail bags.

Situations of this sort can only be avoided by the most bald-faced subterfuge.

First and foremost you must remember that if you have had any contact whatsoever with salt water — other than a gargle — you must conceal it. Even childhood forays to the beach, where you played with your shovel and pail on the seaside sands, should go unmentioned lest it be translated into a suggestion that you are; at heart, an Old Salt — a latency that can be brought to full flower during a single weekend on the *Carrie Mae* or the *C. Mor C.*

Terminology is every sailor's hang-up. Even someone who doesn't even know how to tie a square knot or bail the bilge will nine times out of ten be able to sling around a mouthful of nautical terms that would have a bystander thinking he was in the presence of Popeye.

One of the very best ways to make certain that your landlubbermanship is taken seriously is to forego *ALL* such terms, substituting terra firma equivalents.

Example: You arrive at dockside wearing your golf shoes, and before the skipper even has a chance to notice them, you proudly call his attention to them, lifting first one foot and then the other so he can be sure to see the cleats on the underside.

"Just in case we run into a little rough weather," you tell him. "Some of these green kids you pick up as crew nowadays will go sliding right under the fence if the boat starts jumping around."

A great beginning! By the time he's talked you out of your shoes and into an old, broken-down pair of top-siders minus laces, he'll have begun to have second thoughts. Maybe you're *not* to be so easily converted to the Lore of the Sea.

Assuming this is to be only a one-day sail, it's perfectly understandable that you should arrive with a contribution to the larder. For this we strongly suggest a five-pound bag of unshelled peanuts. Any right-minded skipper will blanch at

the idea of all those peanut shells sliding down behind the seat cushions, getting under the floorboards of the cockpit and in all the myriad unreachable nooks and crannies of which a sailboat is composed.

You step aboard, peanuts in hand.

"Better show me the powder room (po-po, men's room, bathroom) before we get going. Just in case."

In this instance you can use any one of dozens of expressions, just as long as you eschew the only word the skipper wants to hear, the "head" or, as a second best, the "can."

Down goes his confidence another notch.

The business of casting off gets underway. Under no circumstances hang back. Instead, get right in there with offers of assistance, but at the same time be exceedingly careful how you word them.

"If there are any ropes you want me to pull, just say the word."

"Want me to thread these snivvies (your hand on the sail slides) into this groove on the center post here?"

"Should I stuff this big tongue depressor (your hand on the battens) into the pocket places on the sail?"

If you've handled your role with any skill at all, by the time you're actually underway the skipper should be mentally reducing his day's voyage by a healthy fraction. Since your objective is (A) never to be invited back again and (B) to salvage as much of this specific day as is possible, we urge you to waste not a single moment consolidating your already favorable situation.

"How about letting me get in there?" you say to the skipper, tugging playfully on the tiller.

Chances are he'll make a few half-hearted protests about wanting to get clear of the dockside area or perhaps of the harbor. This is your clue to persist in a good-natured way.

A friendly tussle, a little horseplay, and with any luck you should end up with the tiller tucked firmly under your arm.

Lie back. Face canted sunward to catch the rays and, incidentally, so that you can be totally oblivious to all traffic in your channel.

Just the sight of you stretched out with your arm possessively wrapped around the vital parts of his expensive toy will reduce the skipper's confidence.

Regardless of the hour, from this vantage point you suggest it's time to knock back a few brews, reaching blindly as you speak for that big bag of peanuts.

Despite your seemingly laid-back, insouciant attitude, it's important that you time your next maneuver with all the precision of a high-wire walker.

With the mainsail and the jib nicely filled, the boat cutting through the water as smooth as you please, sailing straight downwind and with the skipper either going down into the cabin or, better yet, emerging therefrom, a couple of beers in hand, you swing the bow sharply so that the wind catches the leeward side of the sail. The result, of course, is a crashing of the boom from one side of the boat to the other, (since you're laid pretty flat out there's no chance of your getting konked on the head). The boat is very apt to heel alarmingly in a maneuver known as you well know, as *jibing*. Furthermore, if the winds amount to anything at all, the boat may swing broadside to the wind in a maneuver, as you surely remember from your days at Camp Woebegone, known as *broaching*.

All of the above, accomplished in a mere matter of seconds, is accompanied by a lusty call of "*Fore*!!"

Now, unless you've shipped out with a veritable Captain Queeg, you should be relieved of the tiller and allowed to go forward to a dry and sunny spot up just forward of the mast. There you can relax in sunshine and peace for the rest of the sail.

Be careful not to apologize. After all, what went wrong? Don't hesitate to observe and comment on the day's proceedings, choosing your terms with exquisite care.

- The jib is *that little dinky sail out there in front.*
- The bow is the *front,* the stern is the *back.*
- The deck, of course, is the *floor.*
- Sail bags are *laundry bags.*
- The painter is the *lariat.*
- Tacking is the *zig* or the *zag* of zigzagging.

When you finally get back to the dock, assure the skipper that you simply can't remember a pleasanter day.

"And you can count on me to crew for you — anytime. Just name the day!"

If you've handled the situation carefully, that should be the last time you'll have to spend *any* time on the high seas.